101 BEST FAMILY CARD GAMES

ALFRED SHEINWOLD
Illustrated by Myron Miller

Sterling Publishing Co., Inc.   New York

Library of Congress Cataloging-in-Publication Data Available

Published in 1992 by Sterling Publishing Company, Inc.
387 Park Avenue South, New York, N.Y. 10016
© 1992 by Sterling Publishing Co., Inc.
This edition is based upon *101 Best Card Games*
for the Family by Alfred Sheinwold,
published by Sterling Publishing Co., Inc.
Distributed in Canada by Sterling Publishing
% Canadian Manda Group, P.O. Box 920, Station U
Toronto, Ontario, Canada M8Z 5P9
Distributed in Great Britain and Europe by Cassell PLC
Villiers House, 41/47 Strand, London WC2N 5JE, England
Distributed in Australia by Capricorn Link Ltd.
P.O. Box 665, Lane Cove, NSW 2066
Manufactured in the United States of America
All rights reserved

Sterling ISBN 0-8069-8635-2

Contents

Why Family Card Games?

My own experience makes me feel that every family will benefit from playing card games together.

It is, first of all, fun—and a splendid way to enjoy spending time in each other's company. It's also a great way to get to learn how each other's mind works, which can be important to both parent and child.

Then, too, it's a healthy experience for a child to play with grownups as an equal. It adds to a child's self-esteem when he or she feels included and part of the fun—to say nothing of the implied supposition that the child is intelligent enough to learn the games and worthy of playing them with experienced competitors.

Another major benefit is that the child gets practice in losing without squawking and winning without crowing. (Many adults could use some of this practice, too!)

A young child also can learn about numbers and easy arithmetic from card games. And people of any age can exercise their brain by the logical thinking needed in the more advanced games.

My thanks are due to my old friend Geoffrey Mott-Smith, who worked with me on this book, and to his children for the many games we played together.

**For meanings of terms,
see page 126.**

1.
For the Family with Very Young Children

These games are for children who are too young to think—and for grownups who would rather *not* think! Sometimes it's hard to tell whether the children or the grownups laugh harder!

Pig

This is a very hilarious game for children or for adults to play with children. Anybody can learn it in two or three minutes, and one extra minute makes you an expert!

Players: 3 to 13—5 or 6 make the best game.
Cards: 4 of a kind for each player in the game. For example, 5 players would use 20 cards: 4 Aces, 4 Kings, 4 Queens, 4 Jacks, and 4 10s. For 6 players you would add the 9s.

The Deal: Any player shuffles and deals four cards to each player.

To Win the Game: Get four of a kind in your own hand, or be quick to notice it when somebody else gets four of a kind.

The Play: The players look at their cards to see if they were dealt four of a kind. If nobody has four of a kind, each player puts some unwanted card *face down* on the table and passes it to the player to the left, receiving a card at the same time from the player to the right.

If, still, nobody has four of a kind, each player once again passes a card to the left and gets a new card from the right.

The play continues in this way until one player gets four of a kind. That player stops passing or receiving cards. Instead, he puts his finger to his nose.

The other players must be quick to notice this, and each of them must stop passing in order to put a finger to his nose. The last player to put a finger to his nose is the *Pig*.

Strategy: In trying to put together four of a kind, you usually start with a pair. For example, suppose you are dealt two Kings, one Queen, and one Ace. Keep the two Kings, and pass either the Queen or the Ace. As soon as you get another King, save all three of them, and pass your fourth card. Sooner or later your fourth King will come in.

Don't get so interested in looking for your own four of a kind that you are blind to what the other players are doing. Keep one eye on everybody else, particularly on those who look very eagerly at the cards they are receiving. The eager player probably has three of a kind and is just waiting for the fourth.

The best *Pig* player I know is a seven-year-old girl who doesn't try very hard to make four of a kind. She always tries to look excited, and talks and squeals as she gets each card, just as though she had three of a kind. While doing all of this, she watches the other players to see which of them are most interested in her and which are interested in their own hands.

She knows that the players who are interested in *her* have *bad* hands, but that those who are thinking about the *game* have *good* hands. So little Lisa knows which players to watch, and she is never caught!

Donkey

This is the same game as *Pig*, except that when you get four of a kind you put your hand face down on the table quietly instead of putting your finger to your nose. You still get a card from your right, but you just pass it along to the left, leaving your four of a kind untouched on the table.

As the other players see what has happened, they likewise put their cards down quietly. The idea is to keep up the passing and the conversation while some player plays on without realizing that the hand has really ended.

If you're the last player to put your cards on the table, you lose the hand. This makes you a D. The next time you lose, you become a D-O. The third time, you become a D-O-N. This keeps on, until finally you become a D-O-N-K-E-Y.

The D-O-N-K-E-Y loses the game, and the winner is the player who has the smallest number of letters.

Donkey Buttons

Equipment: Buttons—one less than there are players.

This is the same game as *Donkey*, except that when you get four of a kind, you shout, "Donkey!" and quickly grab a button from the middle of the table. There is one button less than there are players, so the last player to grab doesn't get a button—and becomes a D. The game continues in this way until somebody becomes a D-O-N-K-E-Y.

At the end of the game, the D-O-N-K-E-Y has to bray *"heehaw"* three times.

My Ship Sails

Players: 4 to 7—4 or 5 players make the best game.
Cards: 7 for each player.

The Deal: Any player shuffles and deals seven cards to each player.

To Win the Game: Get seven cards of the same suit.

The Play: Each player looks at his hand and passes one card to the left, receiving at the same time one card from the right. The play goes on in the same way as in *Pig* or *Donkey*. The only difference is that you are trying to collect cards that are all of the same suit.

There are many different ways of ending a hand. When you get seven cards of the same suit, you put your cards down immediately and say, "My ship sails!" Another way is to say nothing but to put your finger to your nose as in *Pig*.

If it takes too long to finish a hand, try one of the shorter games—*My Bee Buzzes* or *My Star Twinkles* (page 10).

Strategy: Begin by trying to collect the suit that you have most of. For example, if you have four or five hearts, pass the other cards and try to collect more hearts.

You may run into trouble if some other player tries to collect the same suit that you are collecting. To guard against this, start collecting a second suit if you don't have any luck with the first. If you can get three cards in a second suit, you can then start to pass the cards of your first suit and switch your plan.

For example, suppose you start with three hearts, two spades, one club, and one diamond. Keep passing the clubs and diamonds until you get another heart or another spade. If you get one more—or a third spade before any heart is passed to you, you may suspect that somebody else is saving the hearts. Your best bet is to break up your hearts and to try to get seven spades instead.

If you have four or more cards in the same suit, it doesn't pay to break. Sit tight and hope that one of the other players will break first and pass the cards that you need.

My Star Twinkles

This is the same as *My Ship Sails* except that you need only five cards of the same suit (and two odd cards) to win a hand. In this game it takes only two or three minutes to play a hand.

My Bee Buzzes

This is the same as *My Ship Sails* except that you need only six cards of the same suit to end the hand. Each player gets seven cards, but needs only six cards in the same suit (and one odd card) to win the hand. It takes less time to finish a hand in this game than in *My Ship Sails*.

Through the Window

Players: 3 to 13—the more the merrier.
Cards: 4 to each player.

The Deal: The dealer shuffles and deals four cards to each player.
To Win the Game: Win the most cards.
The Play: The dealer begins by saying, "I looked through the window and saw. . . ." Just at this moment, and not before, he turns up one of his four cards so that all the players can see it.

Then, each player (including the dealer) must try to say an animal or thing beginning with the same letter of the alphabet as the card that has been turned up. For example, if the card is an Ace, you might call out "Ant," "Alligator,"

"Alaska," or anything else that begins with the letter A. If the card is a 9, you might call out "Nachos" or "Nut."

The first player to call out a correct word takes the card and starts his pile of captured cards separate from the four cards that were dealt to him. Then the person to the left of the dealer says, "I looked through the window and saw . . . ," turning up one of her cards. The game continues in the same way, in turn to the left, until all the cards originally dealt have been turned up and captured. Each person keeps his own pile of captured cards, and the one who captures the most wins the game. The captured cards have nothing to do with each player's original four cards, since each player had exactly four chances to turn up a card.

As soon as a word has been used to win a card, no player can use that same word again. For example, if you have used the word "Stone" to capture a Seven, neither you nor any other player can use the word "Stone" to capture any other card beginning with an S.

Concentration

Players: **Any number at all—the more the merrier.**
Cards: **1 pack.**

The Deal: Spread the cards face down on a table. Don't bother to put them down neatly, but just jumble them up, making sure that no two cards overlap.

To Win the Game: Capture the largest number of cards.

The Play: Before play begins, the players should be told what their turn is, so that they know whether they are first, second, third, and so on.

The first player turns up any card and then turns up any other card. If the two cards match (for example, if they are two Aces or two Kings), the first player captures them as her pair. She then has another turn and proceeds to turn up two more cards in the hope of finding a pair. When she turns up two cards that are not a pair, she must turn them face down again in the same position. It now becomes the turn of the next player.

Strategy: The trick is to remember the cards that have been turned up and exactly where on the table they are. For example, suppose a player turns up a King and a 10. He had to turn those cards face down again. You do your best to remember exactly where that King is and where that 10 is. Then, when it is your turn, you turn up a card on an entirely different part of the table, hoping to find another King or another 10. If you find another King, you can go right to the first King like a homing pigeon and you'll have a pair of Kings to capture. If you find another 10, you can go right to the first 10 and capture those cards, too.

If you try to remember too many cards, you may forget them all. It is much better to begin by trying to remember only two or three cards. When you find that you can do that easily, try remembering four cards. In this way you can gradually increase your skill until you can accurately remember the whereabouts of seven or eight cards at a time. This should be enough to win almost any game.

Tossing Cards into a Hat _____

Players: Any number, but the game is best with two or three.
Cards: 1 old deck—or 2 old decks if playing with more than 3 people.
Equipment: An old felt or straw hat
                   A sheet of newspaper

The Deal: Divide the cards equally among the players.

To Win the Game: Toss the largest number of cards into the hat.

The Play: Place the hat on a sheet of newspaper at the other end of the room, with crown down and brim up.

Standing the whole length of the room away from the hat, each player in turn flips one card towards the hat, with the object of landing the card inside the hat.

Each player keeps track of the cards he has landed inside the hat. If a card lands on the brim, it counts as only one-half a point. If a card on the brim of the hat is knocked in by any player, it counts a full point for the player who originally threw it.

Strategy: The trick is to hold the card between your thumb and forefinger with your wrist bent inwards towards your body. If you then straighten out your wrist suddenly with a flick and release the card at the same time, you can make it sail all the way across a very long room and you can control it pretty well.

Although strength isn't important in this game, small children may have trouble in getting the knack. Allow them to stand several paces closer to the hat.

Special Advice: Be sure to place the hat near a blank wall, and far away from a piano, or a sofa, or any other heavy piece of furniture. Cards that land under a piano are very hard to recover.

Treasure Hunt

Players:	**Any number.**
Cards:	**2 packs.**
Preparation:	**Before the players arrive, hide some of the cards from one deck in one of the**

rooms that you devote to the game. Take out of the second deck cards that match the ones you have hidden. Make sure to hide as many red cards as black ones. A hidden card should be findable without the seeker having to move anything to get to it. For example, if you hide a card in a bookcase, it should be sticking out in some way and not hidden inside any book. Every hidden card should be well within the reach of even the youngest child. It is perfectly fair to put a card under the pedals of a piano, but not on top of the piano where a small child would be unable to see it.

The Play: When the players arrive, appoint two captains and let them choose sides. One team is to find red cards (Hearts and Diamonds), and the other team black cards (Spades and Clubs).

Give each player a card from the second deck and explain that he is to find a duplicate of it, hidden somewhere in a particular room or in two or three rooms, depending on how much space you have for the game. As soon as a player finds the card he is looking for, he is to bring it back to you and get another card to look for. The first team to find all of its hidden cards wins the game.

Be sure to explain that it isn't necessary to move anything in order to find the cards. Mention, also, that anybody who finds a card that she isn't looking for should replace that card in exactly the same spot and tell no one about it. Somebody else will be looking for it, or she herself may be looking for it later on.

This is a good game to play in somebody else's house!

2.
The War Family

Most games of the War family call for the players to keep their eyes open and their brains sharp but don't require great skill in the play of the cards. Skillful players usually win, but even the youngest player has a good chance.

Slapjack

Slapjack is one of the most entertaining games that you can play with a deck of cards. It is one of the very first games that my grandfather taught me, and he didn't complain when I won from him regularly.

Players: 2 to 8. The game is best for 3 or 4 players.
Cards: 1 pack.

The Deal: One at a time to each player until all the cards have been dealt out. It doesn't matter if they don't come out even. The players square up their cards into a neat pile face down in front of them without looking at any cards.
To Win the Game: Win all the cards.
The Play: The player to the dealer's left begins by lifting the top card of her pile and dropping it *face up* in the middle of the table. The next player (to the left of the first player) does likewise—that is, he lifts the top card of *his* pile and drops it face up in the middle of the table, on top of the card that is already there. The play continues in this way, each player in turn lifting the top card of his pile and dropping it face up in the middle of the table.

As soon as any player turns up a Jack, the fun begins. The first player to slap that Jack wins the entire pile of cards in the middle of the table! If more than one player slaps at the Jack, the one whose hand is at the bottom wins the pile.

This means that you have to keep your eyes open and be pretty quick to get your hand down on a Jack. Sometimes your hand is pretty red when you're so quick that another player slaps your hand instead of the Jack, but it's all in fun. Hopefully, grownups are careful not to play too roughly!

I used to beat my grandfather all the time because he would lift his hand high in the air before bringing it down on a Jack, while I would swoop in sideways and could generally snatch the Jack away before his hand even hit the table. Grandpa never seemed to learn!

Whenever you win cards, you must put them face down underneath the cards you already have.

The play goes on until one player has won all the cards. As soon as a player has lost his last card, he may watch for the next Jack and try to slap it in order to get a new pile for himself. If he fails to get that next pile, he is out of the game. Sooner or later, all the players except one are "knocked out" in this way, and the cards all come to one player, who is the winner.

False Slaps: A player who slaps at a card that is *not* a Jack must give the top card of her pile to the owner of the card that she slapped. If the false slapper has no cards to pay the penalty, she is out.

How to Turn Cards: At your turn to play you must lift the top card of your pile and turn it *away* from you as you drop it face up in the middle of the table. This is to make sure that you don't see the card before the other players do. Also, make sure that you let the card go as you drop it on the table.

Strategy: Naturally, you don't want the other players to have a big advantage, so turn the card over very quickly. Then you will see it just about as soon as they do.

Most players use the same hand for turning the cards and for slapping at Jacks. It's a more exciting game, however, if you agree that the hand used for slapping will not be the same hand used for turning the cards.

Some players use the right hand to turn over the card with a quick motion, and they swoop down on the Jack with the left hand. Other experts, since they are much swifter at swooping with the right hand, turn the card over with the left hand. You may have to try it both ways to see which is better for you.

The important thing to remember is that it's better to be a swift swooper than a slow slapper.

Snap

Players: 3 to 8—4 or 5 are best.
Cards: 1 pack.

The Deal: Any player deals one card at a time, until all the cards have been dealt. They don't have to come out even.
To Win the Game: Win all the cards.
The Play: As in *Slapjack,* each player turns up one card at a time at his turn to play. The card must be turned away from the player and dropped on the table, except that each player starts a pile in front of himself for his turned-up cards. For example, in the game for four players, after each player has had a turn, there will be four piles of face-up cards and the four packs of cards face down that were dealt at the beginning.

When a player turns up a card that matches a face-up card on any other pile, the first player to say "Snap!" wins both piles and puts them face down under her own pack.

A player who says "Snap!" at the wrong time, when the turned-up card does not match one of the other piles, must give the top card of his pile to the player who just turned up her card.

As in *Slapjack,* a player who runs out of cards may stay in for the next "Snap!" in the hope of getting a new pile. If she does not win that "Snap," she is out. A player who cries a false "Snap" is out if he has no cards to pay the penalty.
Strategy: Players have to keep looking around to make sure they know which cards are on top of the piles, since these keep changing as the game goes on. They must be ready at all times to shout "Snap!" very quickly. If two or more players begin the word at the same time, the player who ends the word first, wins. If you're a slow talker, this is no game for you.

My grandmother used to play this game with me. She

preferred it to *Slapjack*—which can become rough. We had to make a special rule once because one little girl who was playing with us said "Snap!" every time a card was turned. She had to pay a penalty card most of the time, but this was more than offset because she won every single pile.

Grandma said this wasn't fair, so we adopted the rule that after three false "Snaps" a player was out.

War

Players: 2.
Cards: 1 pack.

To Win the Game: Win all the cards.
The Play: Each player puts his stack of cards face down in front of him and turns up the top card at the same time. The player who has the higher of the two turned-up cards wins both of them and puts them face down at the bottom of his stack of cards. The King is the highest card, and the Ace is the lowest. The full rank of the cards is:

(Highest) 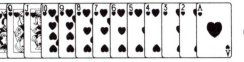 **(Lowest)**

Sometimes *War* is played with the Ace high.

If the two turned-up cards are of the same rank, the players have a "war." Each turns one card face down and then one card face up. The higher of the two new face-up cards takes both piles (a total of six cards).

If the newly turned-up cards again match, there is *double* war. Each player once again turns one card face down and one card face up, and the higher of these two new face-up cards wins the entire pile of ten cards.

95

The game continues in this way until one player has all of the cards.

This is a good game to play when you have a lot of time and nowhere to go.

War for Three

The Deal: When three players want to play *War*, take any card out of the deck and give 17 cards to each.

The Play: For the most part, the play is the same as in two-handed *War*, but when two cards turned up are the same, all three players join in the war by turning one card face down and one card face up. If two of the new turned-up cards are the same, all three players must once more turn one card down and one card face up. As usual, the highest card wins all cards that are used in the war.

If all three turned-up cards are the same, the players must engage in double war. Each player turns two cards face down and then one card face up. If the result is a tie, all three players engage in single war.

Beat Your Neighbor Out of Doors

Other Names: **Beggar My Neighbor**
Strip Jack Naked
Players: 2.
Cards: 1 pack.

The Deal: Give each player half the deck.
To Win the Game: Win all the cards.
The Play: The non-dealer puts a card *face up* in the middle of the table. If it is an ordinary spot card (from the deuce

up to the 10), the dealer covers it with a card from the top of his pile. This process continues, each playing one card in turn on top of the pile, until one of the players puts down an Ace, King, Queen, or Jack.

The moment an Ace or picture card appears, the other player must pay out the proper number of cards, one at a time, face up:

> **For an Ace, four cards.**
> **For a King, three cards.**
> **For a Queen, two cards.**
> **For a Jack, one card.**

If all the cards put down for payment are spot cards, the owner of the Ace or picture card takes up the entire pile and puts it at the bottom of his stack. This is the way the cards are won, and the object of the game is to win all of them.

If, however, you turn up an Ace or picture card while you are paying out to your opponent, the payment stops and he must now pay *you* for the card that you have put down. This process continues, since either player may turn up an Ace or picture card while making a payment. Eventually, however, a player turns up only spot cards in payment, and then the entire pile is lost.

Animals

Players: 3 or more. The best game is for 5 or 6.
Cards: 1 pack.

The Deal: One card at a time until the entire deck has been dealt. It makes no difference if the cards don't come out even.

To Win the Game: Win all the cards.

The Play: Each player takes the name of an animal, such as pig, kangaroo, rhinoceros, hippopotamus.

When everybody fully understands which player represents which animal, the play begins. The player to the dealer's left turns up a card and then each player in turn turns up a card. As in *Snap*, the action takes place when a card that has just been turned up matches some other card that is face up on somebody's pile.

The players who own the matching cards must each call out the animal that the *other* represents. The first to say the other's animal name three times wins both piles.

For example, suppose three players have adopted the names Goat, Pig, and Elephant. The first turns up a Queen, the next turns up a 10, and the third turns up a Queen. The first and the third go into action, but the second must keep silent. The first shouts, "Elephant, Elephant, Elephant!" and the third shouts, "Goat, Goat, Goat!" Both piles are won by the player who finishes talking first.

Play continues until one player has all the cards.

Strategy: When some other player is about to turn up a card, make sure that you have firmly fixed in your mind the card that is at the top of your turned-up pile. And be ready to call out the other person's animal if he matches it.

When it is your own turn to turn up a card, make sure that you have looked at each of the other turned-up cards so that you can instantly spot it if you match one of them. Nine-tenths of the skill in this game lies in being alert.

As you may have noticed, it takes longer to say "Elephant, Elephant, Elephant" than it does to say "Goat, Goat, Goat." For this reason, it always pays to give yourself a long animal name rather than a short one. The longer it takes an opponent to say it three times, the better for you.

Good names to use are: hippopotamus, rhinoceros, elephant, mountain lion, boa constrictor, and so forth.

Farmyard

This is the same game as *Animals,* except that the players go by the noises made by a few farmyard animals instead of by the names of the animals themselves. For example, a player who chose Cow would be called "Moo-Moo-Moo" rather than "Cow, Cow, Cow." A player who chose a Duck would be called "Quack-Quack-Quack," and a player who chose Cat would be called "Meow-Meow-Meow," and so on.

I Doubt It

Other Name: Cheat
Players: 3 or more.
Cards: Use a single pack for 3 or 4 players. Shuffle 2 packs together for 5 or more players.

The Deal: Two or three cards at a time are dealt so that each player gets an equal number of cards. When only a few cards are left, deal one at a time as far as the cards will go.

To Win the Game: Get rid of all of your cards.

The Play: The player to the dealer's left puts from one to four cards face down in the middle of the table, announcing that she is putting down that number of Aces. The next player puts down one to four cards and announces that he is putting down that number of deuces. The next player in turn does the same thing, stating that he is putting down that number of 3s. The play proceeds in this sequence:

Starting 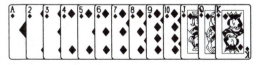 **Ending**

When any player puts down cards and makes his announcement, any other player may say, "I doubt it." The doubted cards must immediately be turned face up. If the statement was true, the doubter must take the entire pile into his hand. If the statement was false, the player who made the false statement must take the pile.

When the players are using two packs shuffled together, a player may put down any number of cards from one to eight.

When a player puts his last cards on the table, some other player must say, "I doubt it," since otherwise the game ends automatically. If the statement turns out to be true, the player wins the game.

A player who has no cards at all of the kind that she is supposed to put down is not allowed to skip her turn. She must put down one or more cards anyway and try to get away with her untruthful announcement. If somebody doubts her claim, she will have to pick up the pile.

If two or more participants say "I doubt it" at the same time, the one nearest the player's left wins the tie; that is, he picks up the pile if the statement turns out to be true after all.

Three-Card I Doubt It

The Deal: The cards are dealt out equally as far as they will go. Put any remaining cards face down in the middle of the table.

The Play: Each player in turn puts down exactly three cards. Instead of starting with Aces automatically, the first player may choose any denomination at all. For example, she may say, "Three 9s." The next player must say, "Three 10s," and so on. When a player has one or two cards left, he must draw enough cards from those put face down in the middle of the table to make up a total of three.

3.
The Authors Family

In all of these games the object is to *match* cards in pairs or sets of four of a kind. A good memory will help you in some of the games, but you can have a hilarious time even if you can hardly remember your own name!

Go Fish

Players: 2 to 5.
Cards: 1 pack.

The Deal: If only two play, deal seven cards to each. If four or five play, deal five cards to each. Put the rest of the pack face down on the table, forming the stock.

To Win the Game: Form more "books" than any other player. A book in this game is four of a kind, such as four Kings, four Queens, and so on.

The Play: The player to the dealer's left begins by saying to some other player, "(Jane), give me your *9s*." He *must* mention the name of the player he is speaking to, and he *must* mention the exact rank that he wants (Aces, Kings, Queens, etc.), and he *must* have at least one card of the rank that he is asking for.

The player who is addressed must hand over all the cards he has in the named rank, but if he has none, he says, "Go fish!"

When told to "go fish," a player must draw the top card of the stock. The turn to ask then passes to the player to his left.

If a player succeeds in getting some cards when she asks for them, she keeps her turn and may ask again. She may ask the same player or some different player, and she may ask for any rank in her new question.

If a player who has been told to "go fish" picks a card of the rank he has asked for, he shows this card immediately before putting it into his hand, and his turn continues. (In some very strict games, a player's turn would continue only if the card he fished for completed a book for him.)

Upon getting the fourth card of a book, the player shows all four, places them on the table in front of him, and continues his turn.

If a player is left without cards, she may draw from the stock at her turn and ask for cards of the same rank as the card that she has drawn. After the stock has been used up, a player who has no cards is out of the game.

The game ends when all 13 books have been assembled. The player with the most books wins.

Strategy: When a player asks for cards and gets them but does not put down a completed book, you can tell that he has either two or three of that rank. For example, suppose John requests Queens and gets one Queen from the player he has asked. John does not put down a book of Queens, but asks some new question and is told to "go fish." You now know that John held at least one Queen to give him the right to ask for Queens. He has received a Queen, which gives him a total of either two or three Queens.

In the same way, you know something about a player's hand when she asks for a card and gets nothing at all. For example, suppose Laura asks somebody for 9s and is told to "go fish" at once. You know that Laura must have at least one 9 in her hand.

Little by little, you can build up information about the cards the other players are holding. If you know that another player has Queens, but you have no Queens yourself, the information does you no good. If you have a Queen yourself, however, you are then allowed to ask for Queens, and if you ask the right person because of the information you have, you may get as many as three cards and be able to put down an entire book in front of you.

Fish for Minnows

This is a simpler way of playing *Go Fish*, and it is especially good for very young players.

The Deal: Deal out all the cards, not worrying about it if they don't happen to come out even.

The Play: At his turn, a player asks for a rank, and the player who has been asked must hand over one such card, if he has one. The object is to form pairs instead of books of four. As soon as a player gets a pair, he puts them face down in front of him.

To Win the Game: Accumulate the most pairs.

Authors

Players: 2 to 5.
Cards: 1 pack.

This game is a lot like *Go Fish,* but it can be played very seriously and with great skill.

The Deal: All 52 cards are dealt out, even though they may not come out even.

The Play: At her turn, a player asks for a single card by naming both its rank and its suit. For example, she might say, "Bill, give me the Jack of Spades." Her turn continues if she gets the card she asked for, but it passes to the left as soon as she asks for a card that the player doesn't hold.

To Win the Game: Win more books (4 cards of the same rank) than any other player.

Old Maid

Other Name: Queen of Spades
Players: 2 or more.
Cards: 51, including only 3 of the 4 Queens. Remove 1 Queen from the pack before beginning the game.

The Deal: One card at a time is dealt to each player, as far as the cards will go. It doesn't matter if the cards don't come out even.

To Win the Game: Avoid getting "stuck" with the last unpaired Queen.

The Play: Each player assorts his cards and puts aside, face down, all cards that he can pair—two by two. For example, he might put aside two Kings, two Queens, two Jacks, and so on. If he had three Queens and three Jacks, he would be allowed to put two of them aside, but the third Jack would stay in his hand.

After each player has discarded his paired cards, the dealer presents her cards, fanned out but face down, to the player at her left. The player at the left selects one card (blindly, since the hand is presented face down) and quickly examines it to see if it pairs some card still in his hand. If so, he discards the pair. In any case, this player now fans his cards out and presents them face down to the player at his left.

This process continues, each player in turn presenting his hand, fanned out and face down, to the player at the left. Eventually, every card will be paired except one of the three Queens. The player who is left with the odd Queen at the end of the hand is the "Old Maid."

Whenever a player's last card is taken, he drops out. He can no longer be the "Old Maid."

Strategy: *Old Maid* can be learned in about one minute, and nothing you can do will improve your chance of winning. The player who is stuck with an odd Queen during the middle of the play usually looks worried and will often squeal with delight if the player to his left selects the Queen. If you keep alert, you can usually tell which player at the table has an odd Queen as the play is going on.

If you have the odd Queen, put it somewhere in the middle of your hand when you present it to the player at your left. Most players tend to pick a card from the middle rather than the ends. Make use of this same principle to defend yourself if you think that the player at your right has the odd Queen when he presents his hand for you to make your choice. He will usually put the Queen in the middle somewhere, and you can usually avoid choosing it by taking one of the two end cards instead.

It isn't bad to get an odd Queen towards the beginning of the play, for you will have many chances to get rid of it. It will then probably stay in some other player's hand or move only part of the way around the table.

If you like to cause a little confusion, act worried when you don't really have the Queen in your hand. Another idea is act delighted when the player to your left picks some perfectly harmless card. This will make the other players in the game believe that he has taken the odd Queen from you. You yourself will usually know where the odd Queen really is, but the other players may be in considerable doubt.

4.
The Stops Family

The many games of the *Stops* family are all good fun, all easily learned, and all suitable for mixed groups of children and adults.

The simplest game of the group has no Stops at all, but it belongs in the family as a sort of great-grandfather of the other games. This game, called *Sequence*, is excellent for very young children.

Sequence

Players: 2 to 10—4 or 5 players make the best game.

Cards: 1 at a time to each player until the deck is used up. It doesn't matter if some of the players are dealt more cards than the others.

To Win the Game: Get rid of all of your cards.

The Play: The player to the dealer's left puts down his lowest card in any suit he chooses. The rank of the cards is:

(Highest) [A K Q J 10 9 8 7 6 5 4 3 2 of clubs] (Lowest)

After the first card has been put down on the table, whoever has the next highest card in the same suit must put it down. This process continues until somebody finally plays the Ace of that suit.

For example, suppose that the first player's lowest Spade is the 4. He puts the 4 of Spades down on the table. Somebody else plays the 5 of Spades, and another player puts down both the 6 and the 7 of Spades (it doesn't matter if the same person plays two or more cards in a row). This process continues until somebody finally plays the Ace of Spades.

When the Ace is reached, the one who plays it must begin a new suit. As before, the player who begins the suit must begin with her lowest card in that suit.

Sooner or later, one of the players will get rid of all of his cards. He wins the hand, and the other players lose one point for every card they still have when the hand comes to an end. (A simpler method is to forget the scoring by points and just play to win the hand.)

Strategy: Practically no skill is required for this game. It

ou do this by getting rid of all your cards or by playing a
ay card so you can win the counters that are placed on it.

he Auction: The dealer looks at his own hand and an-
ounces whether or not he will auction off the extra hand. If
e dealer wants the extra hand himself, he puts his own
and aside, face down, and plays the extra hand in its place.
 the dealer likes his own hand, he is allowed to auction off
e extra hand to the player who bids the most counters for
 If two players make the same bid, the first one to speak
ins. If both speak at the same time, the one who would
ay first going around to the left from the dealer wins the
e. Once the dealer says he is going to sell the extra hand, he
 not allowed to change his mind.

he Play: The player to the left of the dealer must put
own the lowest card of the suit he chooses. The player with
e next higher card in the same suit continues, and the play
oceeds as in *Sequence*. When any player puts down a card
at is the same as one of the pay cards in the middle of the
ble, he collects all the counters on that card. It is therefore
 advantage to hold one of these pay cards in your hand.

If a player reaches the Ace of a suit, she must start a new
it and play the lowest card she holds in that suit.

There is an important difference between this game
d *Sequence*. You cannot always proceed up to the Ace of a
it, because you are sometimes stopped by the missing
rds that are in the discarded hand. When no one is able to
ntinue with a suit, the person who made the last play
ust begin again with a new suit, beginning (as always)
th the lowest card he has in this new suit.

Sooner or later, some person plays the last card in his
nd. He then collects a counter for every card left in the
her players' hands.

rategy: There is skill both in the auction and in the play.
good hand contains one or more pay cards. Even if you
ve no pay cards, you may still have a good chance to play

is wise, though, to begin with the deuce of some sui
is your turn to begin a play. If you have no deuce, be
a 3, or with the lowest card of any suit in your ha
don't follow this policy, you may eventually get stu
deuce or a 3 in your hand.

The great value of this game for very young cl
that it is very easy to teach and children get pr
recognizing numbers and learning how they fol
other in sequence. For especially young children,
want to remove the picture cards from the decl
only the cards from 1 to 10. In this case, of course,
the lowest card, and 10 is the highest card of eacl

Newmarket

Players:	**3 to 8.**
Cards:	**1 pack, plus 4 special "pay card another deck: the Ace of Hearts, King of Clubs, the Queen of Dia and the Jack of Spades.**
Equipment:	**A bunch of counters—poker chi matchsticks, toothpicks, beans,**
Preparation:	**Place the pay cards in the midd table, where they remain throug game. Give each player the sam of counters. Each player puts on ter on each of the pay cards.**

The Deal: The dealer gives one card at a time fa
each player, but also deals one extra hand, as th
were one more player at the table. It doesn't ma
hands have one extra card in them.

To Win the Game: Win counters from the otl

out quickly if your hand contains few very low cards. It usually isn't hard to reach Queens, Kings, and Aces, but it is often very hard to get rid of deuces and 3s.

As the dealer, you may be satisfied with your hand if you have one or more pay cards, or if you have a hand that contains practically no deuces or 3s. If you have a bad hand—no pay cards and two or more very low cards—exchange your hand for the extra hand.

Follow the same principle if some other player is the dealer and offers to auction off the extra hand. The extra hand isn't worth a single counter to you if you already have a good hand. If you have a bad hand, however, it is worth bidding up to three or four counters for the extra hand. If very few players are interested in bidding for the extra hand, you may get it for only one or two counters, but it probably won't be worth much. If the other players are satisfied with their hands, it is probably because they have pay cards, which means that there will be none left in the extra hand. However, there will still be an advantage in exchanging your original hand, because you will be the only player in the game who knows what cards are in the discarded hand.

In the play of the cards, it sometimes helps a great deal to know when a suit is going to be stopped. For example, suppose you know that the 9 of Spades is in the dead hand. If you have the 8 of Spades in your new hand, you can safely begin Spades rather than some other suit. When you eventually play your 8 of Spades, the suit will be stopped, and you will then be able to switch to some new suit. This gives you two chances to play, so it is always an advantage to be the one who switches to a new suit.

When it is up to you to start a new suit, it is usually a sound idea to begin a suit in which you have a pay card. This is your best chance to get the pay card out of your hand and to collect the counters for playing it.

Snip, Snap, Snorem _____

Players: 3 or more—the more the merrier.
Cards: 1 pack.

The Deal: One at a time to each player, until the entire pack is used up. It doesn't matter if some players have more cards than the others.

To Win the Game: Get rid of all of your cards.

The Play: The player to the dealer's left puts any card face up on the table. The next player to the left matches the play with the same card in a different suit, saying "Snip." The next player to the left continues to match the original play with the same card in a third suit, saying "Snap." The next player follows with the fourth card of the same kind, saying "Snorem." If a player is unable to follow with a matching card, he says "Pass," and his turn passes to the next player to the left.

For example, let's say the first player puts down a 6 of Hearts. The next player to the left has no 6 and therefore must say "Pass." The next player has the 6 of Diamonds and puts it down, saying "Snip." The next player to the left has both of the remaining 6s and therefore puts them down one at a time, saying "Snap" for the first one and "Snorem" for the second.

The player who says "Snorem," after putting down the fourth card of a kind, plays the first card of the next group of four. If he has more than one of a kind, he must put down as many as he has instead of holding out one of the cards for "Snorem." For example, if you have two Kings, you must put both of them down if you decide to play a King. You are not allowed to put down just one of the Kings and wait for the other two Kings to appear before showing your remaining King for a "Snorem."

The first player to get rid of his cards wins the game.

The Earl of Coventry

This is the same as *Snip, Snap, Snorem* except that different words are used. The exact word depends on whether the player is young or grownup.

Young children always use the same words when putting down their cards. For example, suppose a young player puts down a 5. He says, "There's as good as 5 can be." The next young player to put down a 5 can say, "There's a 5 as good as he." The next player says, "There's the best 5 of all the three." The fourth player would say triumphantly, "And there's the Earl of Coventry!"

Grownup players need to make a different rhyming statement as they play their cards. For example, an adult who plays a 5 might say, "Here's a 5 you can have from me," or "The best 5 now on land or sea," or any other rhyme.

If a grownup fails to make an acceptable rhymed statement when he plays his card, he is not allowed to begin a new play. The turn passes to the player at his left.

Jig

This is the same as *Snip, Snap, Snorem* or *The Earl of Coventry*, except that the players put down four cards in sequence instead of four of a kind.

For example, suppose that the player to the left of the dealer begins by putting down a 5. The next player must put down any 6 or must pass. The next player must put down any 7 or pass. The play is completed by the next person who puts down any 8. The one who completes the play with the fourth card in sequence then begins the new series.

The game may be played by saying "Snip, Snap, Snorem," or with rhymes, as in the *Earl of Conventry*.

Crazy Eights

Other Name:	Rockaway
Players:	2 to 8. The game is best for 2, 3, or 4. In the 4-handed game, the players who sit across the table from each other are partners.
Cards:	7 to each player in a 2-handed game; 5 to each player when more than 2 are playing.

The Deal: After the correct number of cards is dealt to each player, put the rest of the cards on the table face down as the stock. Turn the top card face up to begin another pile.

The Play: The player to the left of the dealer must match the card that has been turned up. That is, he must put down a card of the same suit or of the same rank.

For example, suppose that the card first turned up is the 9 of Spades. The first player must put down another Spade or another 9.

The newly played card is placed on top of the turned-up card. It is up to the next player to match the new card either in suit or in rank.

The four 8s are wild; that is, you may play an 8 at any time, when it is your turn. When putting down an 8, you are allowed to call it any suit at all, as you please. For example, you might put down the 8 of Hearts and say "Spade." The next player would then have to follow with a Spade.

If, at your turn, you cannot play, you must draw cards from the top of the stock until you are able to play or until there are no more cards left. You are allowed to draw cards from the stock, at your turn, even if you are able to play *without* drawing. This is sometimes a good idea.

To Win the Game: Get rid of all of your cards. The first player to get rid of all of his cards wins.

Sometimes a hand ends in a block with nobody able to play, and with nobody having played out. The hand is then won by the player with the smallest number of cards. If two or more players tie for this honor, the hand is declared a tie.

Strategy: The most important principle is not to play an 8 too quickly. If you waste an 8 when you are not really in trouble, you won't have it to save you when the going gets tough.

The time that you really need an 8 to protect yourself is when you have been *run out of a suit*. For example, after several Spades have been played, you might not be able to get another Spade even if you drew every single card in the stock. If you are also unable to match the rank of the card that has been put down, you may be forced to pick up the entire stock before your turn is over. From here on, of course, it will be very hard for you to avoid a disastrous defeat. An 8 will save you from this kind of misfortune, since you can put it down in place of a Spade, and you may be able to call a suit that does for your opponent what the Spade would have done for you!

If you're lucky, you won't have to play an 8 at the beginning, and you can save it to play as your last card. If you're not quite as lucky as this, it is sensible to play the 8 as your next to last card. With a little luck, you will then be able to play your last card when your next turn comes—and win the hand. To play an 8 with more than two cards in your hand is seldom wise. It is usually better to draw a few cards from stock in order to find a playable card.

The best way to beat an opponent is to run her out of some suit. If you have several cards in one suit, chances are your opponent will be short in that suit. As often as you get the chance, keep coming back to your long suit until your opponent is unable to match your card. Eventually, she will have to draw from stock and may have to load herself up badly before she is able to play.

Hollywood Eights _____

Equipment: Paper and pencil for scoring.

This is the same as the original game of *Crazy Eights*, except that a score is kept in points with pencil and paper. When a hand comes to an end, each loser counts up his cards as follows:

Each 8	**50**
Each King, Queen, Jack, or 10	**10**
Each Ace	**1**
Each other card	**its face value**

The winner of a hand gets credit for the total of all points lost by the other players.

For example, suppose you have an 8, a 9, and a 7 when a hand ends. The 8 counts 50 points, the 9 counts 9, and the 7 counts 7. The total is 50 + 9 + 7, or 66 points.

Hollywood scoring: Three separate game scores are kept. The first time a player wins a hand, his score is credited to him in the first game score. The second time a player wins a hand, he gets credit for his victory both in the first game and also in the second game. The third time a player wins, his score is credited to him in all three games. He continues to get credit in all three games from then on.

Sometimes the game runs on until everybody feels like stopping. In this case, the three game scores are added whenever everybody wants to stop. The winner is the player with the biggest total for the three scores.

Suppose you win five hands in a row, with scores of 10, 25, 40, 20, and 28 points. Your score would look like this:

FIRST GAME		SECOND GAME		THIRD GAME	
	10		25		40
(+25)	35	(+40)	65	(+20) 60	
(+40)	75	(+20)	85	(+28) 88	
(+20)	95	(+28)	113		
(+28)	123				

100 Scoring: A more popular method is to end a game as soon as any player's score reaches 100. When this happens in the first of the three games, the other two games continue. In the later hands, the score is entered on the second game and third games, but no further entry is made in the finished first game. Sooner or later, some player reaches a score of 100 in the second game, and this likewise comes to an end. Eventually, also, some player reaches a score of 100 in the third game, and then all three games have ended.

The winner is the player with the highest total score when all three game scores have been added up.

Go Boom

Players: 2 or more.
Cards: 1 pack.

The Deal: Seven cards are dealt to each player. The rest of the pack is put face down in the middle of the table.
To Win the Game: Get rid of all of your cards.
The Play: The player to the left of the dealer puts any card on the table. The next player to her left must follow by matching the suit or rank of that card. Each player in turn after this must match the previous card in suit or rank.

For example, suppose the first player puts down the Jack of Diamonds. The next player may follow with any Diamond or with another Jack. If the second player decides to follow with the Jack of Clubs, the third player may then match with a Club or with one of the two remaining Jacks.

When a player cannot match the previous card, he must draw cards from the stock until he is able to play. If a player uses up the stock without finding a playable card, he may say "Pass," and his turn passes to the next player.

When everybody at the table has had the chance to play or say "Pass," the cards are examined to see who has played the highest card. The cards rank as follows:

(Highest)  **(Lowest)**

The player who put down the highest card has the right to begin the next play. If there is a tie for first place among cards of the same rank, the card that was played first is considered higher.

The play continues in this way until one player gets rid of all of her cards. That player wins the hand.

If none of the players is very young, you might want to use a system of point scoring. When a hand comes to an end, each loser counts the cards left in his hand as follows:

Each picture card	**10**
Each Ace	**1**
Each other card	**its face value**

The winner of the hand is credited with the total of all points lost by the other players.

Strategy: The strategy in *Go Boom* is much the same as in *Crazy Eights*. You try to run your opponent out of a suit in hopes that he will not be able to match your play with a card of the same suit or the same rank.

In the early stages of play, it is useful to play as high a card as possible in order to have the best chance to win the privilege of beginning the next play.

Hollywood Go Boom

This is the same as *Go Boom*, except that the scoring is Hollywood style (three games at a time). As in *Hollywood*

Eights, three game scores are kept for each player. The first time you win a hand, you get credit only in your first game score. The second time you win a hand, you get credit both in your first game score and in your second game score. After that, you get credit in all three game scores.

The first game ends when any player reaches a score of 100. Later hands are scored only in the second and third games. The second game also ends when any player reaches a score of 100. Thereafter, the scores are entered only in the third game score, and when some player reaches a score of 100 in that game all the scores are totalled to see who wins.

Fan-Tan

Other Names:	**Card Dominoes**	**Sevens**
	Parliament	
Players:	**3 to 8.**	
Equipment:	**A bunch of counters—poker chips, matchsticks, toothpicks, dried beans, etc.**	

The Deal: One card at a time to each player until all the cards have been dealt. It doesn't matter if some players get more cards than others. Give an equal number of counters to each player.

To Win the Game: Get rid of all your cards.

The Play: To open, the player to the left of the dealer must play any 7, if possible. If not, the first player with a 7 opens. After the 7 is played, the next player to the left may play a 7 or any card in the same suit and in sequence with the card previously played.

For example, suppose that the player to the dealer's left put the 7 of Spades on the table. The next player may put down a new 7 or may play the 8 of Spades so that it covers half of the 7 of Spades. The second player, instead, might have chosen to play the 6 of Spades, putting it down also so that it just covered half of the 7 of Spades. If the 8 of Spades were played, the next player would have the right to put down the 9 of Spades. If the 9 of Spades were played, the next player would have the right to put down the 10 of Spades.

This process continues. At any turn, a player may put down a new 7 or may continue a sequence that builds up in suit from a 7 to a King or down from a 7 to an Ace. The King is the highest card that may be played on a sequence and the Ace is the lowest. If a player does not have an appropriate card, he must put a counter into the middle of the table.

The play continues until one player gets rid of all of his cards. That player then collects all the counters in the middle of the table. In addition, each loser pays out one counter for every card left in her hand.

Strategy: It is usually easy to get rid of cards of middle size, such as 8s, 9s, 6s or 5s. It is usually hard to get rid of very low or very high cards, such as Aces and deuces or Queens and Kings.

The best tactic is to force the other players to build up to your high cards or down to your low cards. You can't always carry it off, but you can try.

If you have the 8 of Spades, nobody can play the 9 of Spades or any higher Spade until you have first put down your 8. If a player who has high Spades finds no chance to play them, he must play something else at his turn. This other play may be just what you need to reach your own very low cards or your own very high cards.

This shows you the general strategy. Play as much as possible in the suit that will lead to your very high cards or to your very low ones. Wait as long as possible before playing in the suits in which you have only middle-rank cards.

With just a little luck, you will get rid of your very high cards and your very low cards fairly early. You will then be able to get rid of your middle-rank cards in the last suit, catching the other players while they still have the very high and very low cards in that suit.

Liberty Fan-Tan

This is the same game as *Fan-Tan*, except that it isn't necessary to begin a suit by playing the 7. Nobody can start a new suit until the previous suit has been finished.

The player to the left of the dealer begins by playing any card of any suit. The next player must follow with the next higher card in the same suit or must put one counter in the middle of the table. The third player must continue with the next card in sequence or must put one counter in the middle of the table. This process continues, building up past the King with the Ace, deuce, and so on, until all 13 cards of the suit have been played. The one who plays the 13th card of the first suit may begin with any card in a new suit. Then the same process continues with a second suit.

The first player to get rid of all of her cards takes all the counters from the pool.

Strategy: Your chance of winning is best when you can determine which suit will be played last. If you have very few cards in this suit, you have an excellent chance to win all the counters since you will get rid of your cards while the other players still have cards of that suit left.

The time to choose the last suit does not come after the third suit has been played, since at that point there is no choice. The choice is made after the second suit has been played, since then two suits remain. The player who chooses the third suit automatically fixes the other suit as the fourth.

If you happen to end the second suit, by good luck, you

will then begin the play of the third. Naturally, you should play your longer suit, saving your shorter suit for last.

If the two suits are almost equal in length, it is sometimes wiser to play the shorter suit third and save the other suit for the last. The time to do this is when you have two cards in sequence in the shorter suit. If you start with the higher of these two cards, you will naturally be the one to finish the suit when you play the lower card.

For example, suppose you have a hand with Spades:

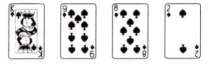

You notice that the 9 and the 8 are in sequence. Following the principle just mentioned, you would begin the suit by playing the 9. Other players would follow with the 10, Jack and Queen, allowing you to play the King. Then someone would play the Ace and you would follow with the 2. The others would then play on until your 8 would complete the suit. Having completed the suit, it is up to you to start the next suit, and this is exactly what you had in mind.

Use the same strategy of starting the second suit with the higher card if you have two cards in sequence. This will allow you to end the second suit and choose the third.

Five or Nine

This is the same as *Fan-Tan* except that the first player may put down a 5 or a 9 (instead of a 7). The card chosen by the first player sets the pattern for the rest of that hand. If he puts down a 5, for example, the other three suits must also begin with 5s; and if the first player begins by putting down a 9, the other three suits must be started by 9s.

Regardless of how the play begins, each suit builds up to a King as its top card and down to an Ace.

Commit

Players: 4 or more
Cards: 1 pack
Equipment: A bunch of counters—poker chips, matchsticks, toothpicks, dried beans, etc.

The Deal: Remove the 8 of Diamonds from the pack. Deal the cards one at a time as far as they will go evenly. Put the remaining cards face down in the middle of the table. Give an equal number of counters to each player.

To Win the Game: Get rid of all your cards.

The Play: The player to the dealer's left may put any card down on the table. She and the other players can then build up in sequence in the same suit.

For example, suppose that Gina begins with the 7 of Clubs. Any player who has the 8 of Clubs puts it face up on the table. Then it is the turn of any player who has the 9 of Clubs. This continues until someone plays the King of Clubs or until the sequence is stopped because the next card is one of those face down in the middle of the table—or the 8 of Diamonds, which has been removed.

When the play stops for either of these reasons, the person who played last begins a new sequence with any card in his hand.

The 9 of Diamonds is a special card in this game. You can of course play it when you end a sequence and it is your turn to begin a new one. But you can also play it in the middle of any sequence. When the 9 of Diamonds is played, each player in turn has the chance to proceed either with the 10 of Diamonds—continuing the Diamond sequence—or with the sequence that was interrupted by the 9 of Diamonds.

For example, suppose that Avery begins a sequence with the 3 of Spades. Barbara puts down the 4 of Spades and then follows it with a 9 of Diamonds. Chris, the player to the left, then has a choice to make. She may continue with a 10 of Diamonds, or go back to the 5 of Spades. If she has neither card, the turn passes on to the left until somebody plays either the 10 of Diamonds or the 5 of Spades, which determines how the sequence will continue.

When you play the 9 of Diamonds, you collect two counters from every player in the game. If anyone gets rid of all of his cards before you have played the 9 of Diamonds, you must *pay* two counters to every player in the game.

When a player wins the game (by playing all his cards), the remaining players must show their hands. Any player who has a King must pay one counter to every other player in the game.

Strategy: As in the game of *Newmarket*, the best strategy is to begin with your lowest card in your longest suit.

It is helpful to remember the stops. At the beginning of a hand, the only stop you are sure of is the 8 of Diamonds. It pays to begin with a low Diamond if you have the 7 of Diamonds in your hand, for then you will probably build up to that 7 and have the chance to begin the next sequence.

Rolling Stone

Players: **4 to 6.**

Cards: **When 4 play, use the Ace, King, Queen, Jack, 10, 9, 8, and 7 of each suit. If there is a fifth player, add the 6s and 5s. If there is a sixth player, add the 4s and 3s. There must be 8 cards for each player.**

The Deal: One card at a time until each player has eight cards. This uses up the pack.

To Win the Game: Get rid of all your cards.

The Play: The player to the dealer's left begins by putting down any card he pleases. Then the play moves to the left and the next player puts down another card in the same suit. The turns continue, always moving to the left, with the other players following with another card of the same suit, if they can, playing high or low, as they please.

If all the cards in a suit are played, the person who put down the highest card leads again. And all the cards that were played to this first "trick" (sequence of cards) are turned over and put aside.

When a player cannot put down a card of the same suit when it is her turn to play, she must pick up all the cards previously played in that sequence. This ends the trick, and the player who picks up the cards then begins the next trick by leading with any card she chooses.

The process continues. In most games a player picks up the cards several times. Eventually, one player will get rid of all his cards, and win the hand.

For the purpose of winning a trick, the cards rank as follows:

(Highest) **(Lowest)**

Play or Pay

Players:	**3 or more**
Equipment:	**A handful of counters—poker chips, matchsticks, toothpicks, dried beans, etc.**

The Deal: One card at a time to each player, until the pack has been used up. It doesn't matter if some players get more cards than others. Give an equal number of counters to each player.

To Win the Game: Get rid of all your cards.

The Play: The player to the left of the dealer may put down any card from her hand. The player to her left must follow with the next highest card in the same suit—or must put a counter into the middle of the table. This process continues, with each player in turn either putting down the next card or paying one counter.

The cards in their proper sequence are:

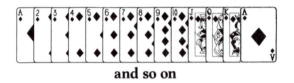

and so on

The player who puts down the 13th card of a suit makes the first play in the next suit.

Keep on playing until someone wins by getting rid of all his cards. Each player then puts one counter in the middle of the table for each card left in his hand. The winner takes all the counters from the middle of the table.

Strategy: There is no skill in following suit; you either have the card or you don't. The only skill is in choosing the right card with which to begin a play.

If you have two cards in sequence in any suit, begin with the one that is higher in rank. Eventually, you will end that suit by playing the lower card of the sequence. This will give you the right to begin the next suit.

When possible, try to get rid of your long suits first.

5.
The Casino Family

Games of the Casino family have been favorites of adults and children for hundreds of years. They are especially recommended by educators because they teach painlessly the first lessons in arithmetic.

Casino

Players: 2 to 4—best for 2.
Cards: 1 pack.

The Deal: The deck of 52 cards is used up in six deals. In the first deal:

> The non-dealer receives two cards face down.
> Then two cards are put face up on the table.
> Then the dealer gives himself two cards face down.

And the process repeats, so that each player and the table have four cards each. In the remaining five deals, the dealer continues to give each player four cards—two at a time—but does not give any additional cards to the table.

The Play: Beginning with the non-dealer, each player in turn must play one card from her hand, until all four of her cards are gone. If she can find no better use for it, she simply lays her card face up on the table. This is called *trailing*. Whenever she can, though, she uses her card to capture cards from the table.

To Win the Game: Get the highest number of points. You get points by capturing the most cards, the most Spades, Aces, the 10 of Diamonds (Big Casino) and the 2 of Spades (Little Casino). See "Scoring."

Pairing: You may win cards in various ways. The simplest is by pairing. You may capture a card on the table by another of the same rank from your hand—a 5 with a 5, a Jack with a Jack, and so on.

With a picture card—a Jack, Queen or King—you may capture only one card, but with a card of lower rank, you may take two or three of the same kind at the same time. If there are two 7s on the table and you have a 7 in your hand, for example, you can take all three 7s.

Each player keeps captured cards in a pile, face down.

Building: All the lower cards, Ace to 10, may be captured by building. Ace counts as 1. Each other card counts as its own value. Cards on the table may be taken in by higher cards to equal their sum.

For example, you may take a 5 and a 2 with a 7—or an Ace and a 9 with a 10. You may, at the same time, take additional cards by pairing. Suppose that the cards on the table are 9, 8, 5, 4, Ace. You could take them all with a single 9, since the 9s pair, 8 and 1 make 9, and 5 and 4 make 9.

Leaving a Build: Suppose that you have 8 and 3 in your hand and there is a 5 on the table. You may put the 3 on the 5 and say, "Building 8." Your intention is to capture the build with your 8 on your next turn. You cannot build and capture in the same turn, because you are allowed to play only one card from your hand at a time.

If your opponent has an 8, she can capture your build. That is the risk of leaving a build. Yet the risk is usually worth taking, because in building, you make it harder for your opponent to capture the cards. She cannot take the 5 or the 3 by pairing or by making a build of her own.

Of course, you may not leave a build unless you have a card in your hand that can take it. You *are*, however, allowed to duplicate your build before taking it in. Suppose you have two 8s in your hand. After building the 5 and 3, you could on your next turn simply put one 8 on the build, and take it with the other 8 on your third turn.

Or suppose after you build the 5 and 3, your opponent trails a 6, and you have a 2 in your hand (besides the 8). You may take your 2 and put it—with the 6—on the 5-3 build and wait until your next turn to take in the duplicated build.

An important rule is that when you have left a build on the table, you must deal with it at your next turn—take it in—or increase or duplicate it. You are not allowed to trail or to take in other cards instead.

Increasing a Build: Suppose that your opponent has laid a 4 from her hand on a 5 on the table and called out, "Building 9." You have an Ace and a 10. You may add the Ace to her build and say, "Building 10." You are allowed to increase a build of your own, in the same way.

But there are two restrictions on increasing a build. First, you may increase only a *single* build, such as the 5-4, not one that has been duplicated in any way, such as 5-4-9. Second, the card you use to increase it must come from your hand; you are not allowed to use a card from the table.

Scoring: After the last card of the sixth deal is played, any cards remaining on the table go to the player who was last to capture cards. Then each player looks through his captured cards and counts his score, as follows:

Cards, for winning 27 or more cards	3 points
Spades, for winning seven or more Spades	1
Big Casino, the 10 of Diamonds	2
Little Casino, the 2 of Spades	1
Aces, each counting 1, total	4
	11

The first one to reach a total of 21 or more points wins.

Spade Casino _____

This is *Casino* with a different count for Spades. Instead of getting one point for having seven or more Spades, the Spades score as follows:

Jack	2
Little Casino	2
Other Spades	1 each

There are 24 points to be won. The game is usually set at 61 and scored on a Cribbage board.

Sweep Casino

This is *Casino* with the additional rule that a player scores one point for each *sweep*. You earn this by capturing all the cards that are on the table at any one time. To keep track of sweeps, turn the top card of each sweep face up.

Winning the cards left on the table after the last deal does not count as a sweep.

Pirate Casino

The "pirate" feature is that you are allowed to make any play you please at a time when you have left a build on the table. You may take in other cards, or even trail.

Stealing Bundles

This is *Casino* for the very young. Cards may be captured only by pairing, but any number of the same kind may be taken at a time. Captured cards must be kept in a pile face up, and you can capture your opponent's entire pile by matching its top card with a card from your hand.

To Win the Game: Win more than half the cards.

Royal Casino

Children often prefer this colorful elaboration on the basic game. Since *Royal Casino* is more complicated, young children should learn the basic game before attempting it.

In this game you may capture face cards as well as lower cards two, three, and four at a turn. Furthermore, they can be used to capture builds:

Jack counts	11
Queen counts	12
King counts	13
Ace counts	14 or 1, as you please
Big Casino	10 or 16
Little Casino	2 or 15

Sweeps are scored, as in *Sweep Casino*.

Partnership Casino

Players: 4, the two opposite being partners.
Cards: 1 pack.

The Deal: The deck is used up in three deals. In the first, each player receives four cards and four are dealt face up on the table. For the other two deals, each receives four more cards, but no more are dealt to the table.

Otherwise, this game is played just like *Casino* (basic or *Royal*), except that you may duplicate a build left by your partner without you yourself having a card that can take it.

For example, if Tom builds 10, Nellie, his partner, may in turn put a 6 from the table and a 4 from her hand on the build, without having a 10 in her hand.

Draw Casino

You can play either basic *Casino* or *Royal Casino* in "Draw" style. After you deal, place the rest of the pack face down in the middle of the table. Each time you play a card, draw the top card of this stock, so that you keep four cards in your hand throughout the game. After the stock is exhausted, play out the hands as usual.

6.
The Rummy Family

Rummy is the most widely played of all card games. Many different forms of the game are played, but all have a very strong family resemblance. Once you have learned to play the basic game, you can pick up any variation in a few minutes.

Basic Rummy

Players:	2 to 6.
Cards:	10 each when 2 play
	7 each when 3 or 4 play
	6 each when 5 or 6 play.
Equipment:	Pencil and paper for keeping score.

The Deal: Deal the appropriate number of cards to each player and then put the rest of the cards face down in the middle of the table, forming the stock. Turn the top card face up, starting the discard pile.

In a two-handed game, the winner of each hand deals the next hand. When more than two play, the turn to deal passes to the left exactly as the cards are dealt out.

To Win the Game: Win points from your opponents. You usually keep track of these points with a pencil and paper score.

In order to win points, you must match up your cards. One way to match is to get three or four of a kind. For example, you might have three Kings or four 10s, and so on.

A second way to match is to get sequences—cards that are next to each other in rank and are in the same suit. The rank of the cards in *Rummy* is:

(Highest) **(Lowest)**

A typical sequence is:

Another typical sequence is:

You need at least three cards for a sequence.

The Play: Each player at the table plays in turn, beginning with the player to the dealer's left. During your turn to play, you do three things:

> **You draw.**
> **You meld (if you wish to do so).**
> **You discard.**

When you draw, you may pick up the top card of the stock or the top card of the discard pile. You add this card to your hand.

You meld by putting a group of matched cards down on the table. For example, you might put down three of a kind or four of a kind, or a sequence. You might even put down two groups of matched cards, if you are lucky enough to have them in your hand. You are not required to expose your meld if you don't wish to do so. You can keep it in your hand.

After some other player has melded, you may add to his meld when it's your turn. For example, if some player has put down three Kings, you may add the fourth King at your turn to play. If some player has put down the 6, 7 and 8 of Diamonds, you may add the 9 and 10 of Diamonds, or just the 9 or the 5 or 5 and 4, or any such card or group of cards. You may add to a meld that has been put down previously by any player at the table—including yourself.

After you have drawn and melded (or after you have declined to meld), it is your turn to discard. You take any card from your hand and put it on top of the face-up pile in the middle of the table. This completes your play.

When, at your turn to play, you manage to meld all your cards, you win the game. You must begin your play with a draw, thus adding one card to your hand, and then you must meld either all the cards in your hand or all but one. If you meld all but one card, that last card is your discard.

If no player has melded all his cards (called *going out*)

by the time the stock is used up, the next player may take either the top card of the discard pile or the top card of the new stock that has been formed by turning the discard pile over. In either case, play continues as before until somebody does go out.

Scoring: The winner of a hand scores points by counting up the hands of all the other players in the game. Each loser counts his cards according to the following scale:

> **Picture cards — 10 points each**
> **Aces   — 1 point each**
> **Other cards — their face value**

A loser does not count cards that he has previously melded on the table, but he does count any cards that remain in his hand—*whether or not these cards match!*

A player goes "Rummy" when he melds all his cards in one turn, without previously melding or adding to anybody else's meld. A player may go "Rummy" by melding all his cards after the draw, or he may meld all but one and then discard that last card. Whenever a player goes "Rummy," he wins double the normal amount from each of the other players.

A score is kept on paper with a column for each player in the game. Whenever a player wins a hand, the amounts that he wins from the other players are put into his winning column.

Some players agree on a stopping time when they play *Rummy*. The winner of a game is the player who has the highest score when the agreed-upon time comes.

Other players end a game when any player reaches a certain total score, such as 500 points.

The score for each player is added up at the end of each hand.

Strategy: In all games of the *Rummy* family, you try to build up your hand by keeping cards that match and by discarding cards that do not match.

For example, if you drew the 10 of Spades, you would tend to keep it if your hand contained one or more 10s, or the Jack of Spades or the 9 of Spades. In such cases, your 10 of Spades might be a useful card. Even if it did not immediately give you a meld, it would probably bring you closer to one.

If you drew a card that did not match anything in your hand, you would either discard it immediately or wait for a later chance to discard it.

If the player to your left picks a card from the discard pile, this gives you a clue to his hand. If, for example, he picks up the 9 of Diamonds, you know that he must have other 9s or other Diamonds in the neighborhood of the 9. If convenient, you would avoid throwing another 9 or another Diamond in that vicinity onto the discard pile. This is called *playing defensively.* You don't need to bother with defensive play against anybody but the player to your left, since your discard would be covered up by the time any *other* player wanted to draw.

The advantage of melding is that you cannot lose the value of those cards even if some other player wins the hand.

The advantage of holding a meld in your hand is that nobody can add to the meld while it is still in your hand. A second advantage is the possibility of going "Rummy" all in one play.

It sometimes pays to hold up a meld, but most successful *Rummy* players make it a habit to put melds down fairly quickly. It is usually safe to hold up a meld for one or two turns, but after that it becomes dangerous. If another player goes out before you have melded, you will lose those matched cards just as though they were unmatched.

Block Rummy

This is the same as *Basic Rummy*, except that the discard pile is not turned over to begin as stock again. When the stock has been used up, the next player has the right to take the top card of the discard pile. If she does not wish to take it, the hand ends immediately. This is called a *block*.

When a block occurs, each player shows his hand. The player with the lowest number of points in his hand wins the difference in count from each of the other players. If two or more players tie for the low number of points, they share the winning equally.

Boathouse Rummy

This is like *Basic Rummy*, except that sequences go "around the corner." For example, you may meld:

as a sequence. But you are not allowed to meld anything at all until you can meld your whole hand and go out. When you go out, you win points from every other player according to his *unmatched* cards—that is, the cards in his hand that he has not matched up in groups of three or four or in sequences.

Scoring: There are two methods. One is to count one point for each unmatched card.

The other is to count

11	for an unmatched Ace
10	for a face card
face value	for all other cards

One other peculiarity of *Boathouse Rummy* is in the draw. When you begin your turn, if you draw the top card of the discard pile, you may then draw a second card—from the discard pile or the stock, whichever you please. If you begin by drawing from stock, however, you don't get a second card.

Contract Rummy

Other Name: **Liverpool Rummy**
Players: **3 to 8.**
Cards: **2 packs of 52 cards plus 1 Joker, for 3 or 4 players.**
3 decks plus 2 Jokers, for 5 or more players.
Equipment: **Paper and pencil for keeping score.**

The Deal: Deal 10 cards to each player, except in Deal 7, when each player receives 12. Put the rest of the cards face down in the middle of the table, forming the stock. Turn the top card of the stock face up beside it, starting the discard pile.

To Win the Game: Get rid of all the cards in your hand by melding them.

Melds: The melds are as in *Basic Rummy*:

groups of three or four cards of the same rank, such as Queens

sequences of three or more cards of the same suit, such as:

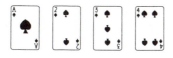 

The Contract: A game consists of seven deals. In each deal, a player's first meld must be a combination of two or three sets according to this schedule:

> **Deal 1: two groups**
> **Deal 2: one group and one sequence**
> **Deal 3: two sequences**
> **Deal 4: three groups**
> **Deal 5: two groups and a sequence**
> **Deal 6: one group and two sequences**
> **Deal 7: three sequences**

When you meld in Deals 1–6, you may put down only three cards per set. If you have additional matching cards, you may put them down at any later turn.

In Deal 7, however, you must meld all 12 cards at once, thus going out.

The Play: As in *Basic Rummy*, a turn consists of a draw, melding (if you wish), and a discard.

If you, the first player, decide not to draw the top card of the discard pile, you must say so. Then any other player who wants it may take it. If two or more want it, the person nearest you (to the left) is entitled to it. He must pay for the privilege of taking the discard out of turn, though, by drawing the top card of the stock also. He must then await his regular turn before melding or discarding. Then you resume your turn, drawing the top card of the stock.

Your first meld of any kind must be the *contract*. After that, you are not allowed to meld any new sets, but you may add matching cards to any sets on the table—yours and the other players'.

A peculiarity of the game is that a sequence may be built to the Ace both ways, making a set of 14 cards. (Of course, this rarely happens.)

Wild Cards: The joker is wild. You may call it any card you please, to help you get rid of cards by melding. You must say, though, what card it represents.

For example, if you put the Joker down with the 7 of Spades and the 7 of Diamonds, you must say either "7 of Hearts" or "7 of Clubs." The reason for this is shown by the next rule. A player who holds the named card may, in her turn, put it down in place of the Joker, thus getting the Joker for her own use.

Many players like to have additional wild cards, to make it easier to form sets for the contract. Deuces are often used as wild, but a deuce cannot be captured, as a Joker can. However, if a deuce is melded in a sequence, any player may put the natural card in its place and move the deuce to either end of the sequence.

Ending Play: Play continues until somebody goes out. If the stock is exhausted, the discard pile is turned over without shuffling.

Scoring: The player who goes out scores zero—which is good! Each other player scores the total of the cards left in his hand. Aces and wild cards count 15 each, picture cards are 10, other cards count their face value. The player with the *lowest* total score after Deal 7 wins the game.

Knock Rummy

Players:	2 to 6.
Cards:	10 cards to each player when 2 play.
	7 cards to each player when 3 or 4 play.
	5 cards to each player when 5 or 6 play.
Equipment:	Paper and pencil for keeping score.

The Play: The play follows *Basic Rummy*, but there is no melding until somebody knocks. To "knock" means to lay down your whole hand face up, ending the play. You may knock in your turn, after drawing but before discarding. You do not have to have a single meld to knock—but you had better be convinced that you have the *low* hand.

When anybody knocks, all players lay down their hands, arranged in such melds as they have, with the *unmatched* cards separate. What counts is *the total of unmatched cards.*

If the knocker has the lowest count, he wins the difference of counts from each other player.

If he lays down a *rum hand*—one with no unmatched card—he wins an extra 25 points from everybody, besides the count of unmatched cards held by the others.

If somebody beats or ties the knocker for low count, that player wins the difference from everybody else.

When the knocker is beaten, he pays an extra penalty of 10 points.

It's best to keep score with paper and pencil. Each item should be entered twice—*plus* for the winner and *minus* for the loser.

Tunk

Players: 2 to 5.
Cards: One pack with 2 or 3 players.
Two packs with 4 or 5 players.

The Deal: Each player receives seven cards.
The Play: The rules follow *Basic Rummy*, and the object is to go out.

Deuces are wild and may be used in place of natural cards to form melds.

To go out, you don't need to meld all your cards, but merely reduce the total of your unmatched cards to five or less. Before going out, you must give notice by saying "Tunk," in your turn—and that is all you can do in that turn. A tunk takes the place of draw-meld-discard. Then the other players unload all that they can from their hands, and on your next turn you lay down your hand, ending the play. You may at any time add cards to your own melds, or to a tunker's melds after the tunk, but not on another player's.

The tunker scores zero, and the others are charged with the count of all cards left in their hands. When a player reaches 100, he is out of the game, and the others play on until there is only one survivor.

Gin Rummy

Gin is one of the best and also one of the most popular of the *Rummy* games.

Players: 2.
Cards: **A regular pack of 52. The ranking is:**

(Highest) 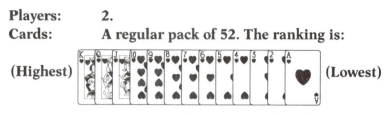 **(Lowest)**

Equipment: **Paper and pencil for keeping score.**

The Deal: Each player receives 10 cards, dealt one at a time. Place the rest of the deck face down in the middle of the table to form the stock. Turn over the top card of the stock beside it. This *upcard* starts the discard pile.

The Play: The non-dealer plays first. If she wants the upcard, she may take it, but if she doesn't want it, she must say so without drawing. Then the dealer may take the upcard, if he wishes, and discard one card from his hand, face up. After he has taken or refused it, the non-dealer continues with her turn, drawing one card—the top card of the stock or the new top of the discard pile. Then she must discard one card face up on the discard pile. The turns alternate and there are no further complications.

To Win the Game: Reduce the count of your unmatched cards.

A "matched set" in *Gin* is the same as a "meld" in *Basic Rummy*—three or four cards of the same rank, or three or more cards in sequence in the same suit. For example, here are two matched sets:

Since, in *Gin*, Aces rank low:

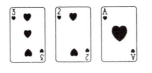 

This is a sequence.   **This is not.**

The point values are:

Ace:	1
Picture cards:	10
Other cards:	face value

Knocking: All melding is kept in the hand until some player brings matters to a halt by laying down all his 10 cards either by "ginning" or by "knocking."

To gin, you lay down all your cards in melds. When you knock, you have unmatched cards whose total is 10 or less. You may knock only when it is your turn to play, after drawing and before discarding. The final discard is made *face down*, thereby indicating the intention to knock. If you simply place the card face up, intending to lay down your hand, you could be stopped, because—according to the rules—the face-up discard ended your turn.

As you play, you arrange your cards in matched sets with the unmatched cards to one side. It is customary to announce the total count of your unmatched cards by saying something like, "Knocking with five," or "I go down for five." Your opponent then exposes her hand, arranged by matched sets and unmatched cards. She is entitled to lay off cards on your sets, provided that you don't have a *gin hand*—all 10 cards matched.

For example, if you had the hand shown on the next page, your opponent could lay off the fourth Jack, and the 10 and 6 of Hearts, if she had any of these cards.

Knock Hand

Scoring: Your opponent counts her remaining un-matched cards, after laying off what she can on your hand. If this count is higher than yours, you win the difference. If your opponent has the same count that you have—or a lower one—she scores the difference (if any), plus 25 points for *undercutting* you.

If you lay down a gin hand, your opponent may not lay off any cards on it. You win the opponent's count, plus a bonus of 25 points. This bonus cannot be won when you knock. Suppose, for example, you play 'possum with a gin hand until your opponent knocks with one point or more. You would win her count, plus 25 for undercutting, but you don't get the bonus for a gin hand.

Keeping Score: Keep score with pencil and paper. Enter the net result of a hand in the column under the winner's name, draw a line below the item, and then write the running total. The lines between items are important, to keep track of how many hands were won by each player.

The first player to reach a total of 100 or more wins the game. You score a bonus of 100 for winning and an additional 100 for a *shutout*—also called "whitewash," "skunk," "Schneider," "goose-egg," etc.—if your opponent has not scored a single point. Then each player is credited with 25 points for each winning hand. This is called the *line* or *box* score. The winner then carries forward the difference between his own grand total and his opponent's.

Hollywood Gin

This is *Gin* with Hollywood scoring (see pages 40–41).

Oklahoma Gin Rummy

This is simply *Gin*, except that the upcard determines the maximum number with which you may knock.

For example, if you turn up a 3 from the stock, it takes 3 or less to knock in that deal.

If you turn up a 10 or a picture card, the game is no different from regular *Gin*. Some players like to pep up the game with additional rules, such as: The hand counts double when the upcard is a Spade.

Around-the-Corner Gin

This is *Gin* again, except that sequences may go "around the corner." For example, this sequence

is a matched set.

An unmatched Ace counts as 15 points. The person who doesn't knock may lay off cards even on a gin hand. The game is usually set at 125 points.

500 Rummy

The chief feature of *500 Rummy* is that you score for melding as well as for going out.

Other Name: **Sequence Dummy**
Players: **3 to 8.**
Cards: **When more than 4 play, use 2 packs of 52 shuffled together.**
Equipment: **Paper and pencil for keeping score.**

The Deal: 7 cards go to each player. The turn to deal passes to the left.

The Play: As in *Basic Rummy*, you may begin your turn by drawing the top card of the stock or the discard pile. But you have a third choice: You may draw *any* card of the discard pile, no matter how deeply it is buried, provided that you immediately meld this card. You must also pick up all the cards that cover it and add them to your hand. You then proceed to meld all the cards you wish to. Your turn ends when you discard.

Discards are not stacked in a pile as in most Rummy games, but are spread out in an overlapping fan so that all the cards can be seen. It is of course important not to mix up the order in which they lie. When you "dig deep" into the discards, courtesy requires that you leave the cards on the table for a while, to give the other players a chance to see what you're getting.

Melds are made as in *Basic Rummy*. You may add cards to your own melds and also to those belonging to other players.

Play ends when some player gets rid of all his cards, with or without making a final discard. If nobody goes out by the time the stock is exhausted, play continues so long as each player in turn draws from the discard pile, but it ends as soon as any player fails to do so.

Scoring: When play ends, each player counts up the difference between the cards he has melded and the cards left in his hand. This difference (which may be plus or minus) is added to his running total score, which is kept on paper.

The cards count as follows:

Ace	15 or 1, if it was melded in a low sequence
Picture cards	10 each
Other cards	face value

The first player to score 500 points wins the game.

Strategy: Much more is won by melding than by going out. Try to meld as much as possible, and to meld high cards rather than low ones. For this purpose, you'll want to get as many cards into your hand as you can. The deeper you have to dig into the discard pile, the happier you'll be!

If you are dealt a low meld, such as three deuces, discard one of them as soon as you can. Then, after the discard pile has grown to 10 or 12 cards, reclaim your deuce to meld it—and get some booty! Just don't be too greedy; if you wait too long, somebody else may take the pile, for you can be sure that the others will "salt" the pile too, if they have the chance.

At the beginning of a game, try to avoid making it too easy for another player to take the discard pile. You may make it easy if you discard a card that pairs with another already in the pile, or that is in suit and sequence with one in the pile. Of course, there comes a time when you have no more safe discards. Then follow the principle of doing the least damage. Discard a card that may let another player take a *few* cards, rather than a great many.

As a rule, don't meld unless you have to in order to dig

into the discard pile. Keeping a meld of high cards in your hand, especially Aces, puts the fellow who has the fourth Ace on the spot. If he discards it, he gives you a chance to pick up the pile; if he holds it, he may get stuck with it. If you meld your Aces, his troubles are over. If you are too lavish in melding, you may help another player go out.

You need to be quick to switch your tactics, however, when the stock is nearly gone or when another player reduces his hand to only a few cards. That's the time to meld your high cards, to be sure that they will count *for* you instead of against you.

7.
Trump Games

A trump suit is one that is given a special privilege: it can take all the other suits. For example, if Spades are trumps, a Spade will win over any Heart, Club, or Diamond. The deuce of Spades then can take the Ace of Hearts, although the Ace of Hearts can win over any lower Heart.

In some games, the trump suit is determined by turning up a card from the deck—its suit becomes trump. In other games, the right to name the trump suit is decided by the players *bidding*. It goes to the player who is willing to pay most for that right. Players *bid* what they are willing to pay—a number of counters to be put in a pool, for example. Usually, each bidder names a number of points or tricks that she hopes to win. The one who names the trump must win at least what she has bid, in order to advance her score. If she fails, points are taken away from her or her opponent's score (according to the particular game). Failing to make a bid goes by different names in different games—"set," "euchre," "bate," and so on.

Linger Longer

A good way to start learning trump games.

Players: 4 to 6.

Cards: Each player receives as many cards as there are players in the game. For example, with 5 players, each receives 5 cards.

The Deal: The last card dealt, which goes to the dealer, is shown to all the players. It decides the trump suit for that trick. The rest of the deck is placed face down in the middle of the table, forming the stock.

The Play: The player to the left of the dealer makes the first *lead* (play), putting down in the middle of the table any card in the trump suit, if he can. Otherwise, he may put down whatever card he pleases. The other players must *follow suit*, putting down any cards in their hand that match the suit of the first lead.

The cards are played in "tricks." Each player tries to capture the trick of four cards by playing the highest trump, or, if there is no trump, by the highest card played of the suit that was led.

When a player wins a trick, he "owns" those cards and draws the top card of the stock. That card determines the trump suit for the next trick. When a player is left without any cards, he has to drop out of the game, and the others play on.

To Win the Game: To get all the cards and be the last player left when everyone else has dropped out. If two or more players are down to one card each at the end, the winner of the last trick wins the game.

Napoleon

Other Name: Nap
Players: 2 to 6.
Cards: A regular pack of 52.
Equipment: A handful of counters—poker chips, matchsticks, toothpicks, dried beans, etc.

The Deal: Each player receives five cards, one at a time. Give out the counters, the same number to each player.

The Bidding: The player to the left of the dealer has the first turn. He "bids" (predicts) the number of tricks he will take if he is allowed to name the trump suit. Each player has one turn in which he may pass or may bid from one to five. A bid of five tricks is called "nap."

The Play: The highest bidder names the trump suit and makes the first lead, which must be a trump.

The cards are played in tricks. The players must *follow suit* to the lead card if they can. Otherwise, there is no restriction on what they may play or lead.

The winner of each trick leads to the next trick—playing any suit—and everyone continues to follow that lead. The trick is won by the highest card.

The bidder tries to win the number of tricks she has named. All the other players combine forces against her. Play stops the moment the outcome is sure—success or defeat for the bidder.

Scoring: When a bidder wins, she collects from each other player the same number of counters as her bid. If she is defeated, she pays this number to each player.

The bid of "nap" for all the tricks is special. If you make it, you collect 10 counters from each player, but if you fail, you pay five to each one.

Loo

Players: 5 to 8 (6 is best).
Cards: A regular pack of 52.
Equipment: A handful of counters—poker chips, matchsticks, toothpicks, dried beans, etc.

The Deal: Each player receives three cards, one at a time. An extra hand of three cards is dealt just to the left of the dealer. This is the *widow*. If the player to the left of the widow does not like her hand, she may throw it away and take the widow instead. If she is satisfied with her hand, though, she must say so and stick with it.

Then each player in turn has a chance to take the widow, until somebody takes it or all refuse it.

Give the same number of counters to each player.

The Play (Single Pool):   After the matter of the widow is settled, the player to the left of the dealer makes the opening lead. You must always *follow suit* to the lead when you can; you must *play higher* than any other card in the trick, if you can. Later, once trump is declared and a plain suit is led of which you have none, you must *trump*, if you can.

The highest trump, or, if there is no trump, the highest card of the suit led, wins the trick. Aces are high.

You must keep the tricks you have won face up on the table in front of you as you play.

Trumps: The play begins without any trump suit and continues that way so long as everybody follows suit to every lead. When somebody fails to follow suit, the top card of the undealt stock is turned over. This card decides the trump suit. The trick just played is examined and if a card that has been played turns out to be trump, that card wins the trick.

Scoring: To start a pool, the dealer must *ante up* three counters. When the pool contains no more than these three counters, it is a *single*, and play takes place as described above. After the play, the pool pays out one counter for each trick won. Players who have not won a trick must pay three counters into the next pool, making it a *double*—or jackpot.

Double Pool: This is formed by the dealer's ante of three plus any payments for *loo* (not winning a trick in the previous hand). After the deal, the next card of the deck is turned up, deciding the trump suit. After checking out their hands, the players must say in turn whether they will play or drop out. If all but the dealer drop out, he takes the pool. If only one player ahead of the dealer decides to play, the dealer must play, too. He may play for himself—in which case he cannot take the widow—or he may play to "defend the pool," in which case he must throw away his hand and take the widow. When the dealer plays merely to "defend the pool," he neither collects nor pays any counters; the pool settles with his opponent alone.

The nearest active player to the left of the dealer leads first. The other rules of play are the same as in a single pool.

The double pool pays out one-third of its contents for each trick won. A player who stays in and does not win a trick must pay three counters to the next pool.

To Win the Game: Win the largest number of counters.

Rams

Players: **3 to 5.**

Cards: **A pack of 32. Discard all 2s to 6s from a regular pack of 52. The cards rank:**

(Highest)      **(Lowest)**

Equipment: **A handful of counters—poker chips, matchsticks, toothpicks, dried beans, etc.**

The Deal: Each player receives five cards in batches of three and two. An extra hand or *widow* is dealt, as in *Loo*. The last card belonging to the dealer is exposed to determine the trump suit.

Give the same number of counters to each player.

Declaring: After looking at their hands, the players in turn must declare whether they will play or drop out. If they play, they must undertake to win at least one trick. Any player in turn may discard the hand and take the widow instead (if it has not yet been taken).

Any player may declare *rams*—undertake to win *all* the tricks. This declaration may be made either before or after taking the widow, but it must be made before the next player has declared. In a *rams* game, everybody must play; players who have dropped out must pick up their hands again. If the rams player has not taken the widow, each player who has not refused it gets a chance to take it.

The Play: The player who declared rams makes the opening lead. Otherwise, it is made by the first player to the left of the dealer.

You must follow suit when you can, and you must play higher than any previous card in the trick, when you can. If a plain suit is led, you have to trump if you are able to, even if the trick has already been trumped. You must trump higher if you can. A trick is won by the highest trump in it, or, if no trump, by the highest card of the suit led.

Scoring: The dealer antes up five counters. The pool may contain counters left from the previous deal.

Each player who has stayed in the game takes one counter (or one-fifth of all the counters) from the pool for each trick he wins. Players (as in *Loo*) who win no tricks must pay five counters into the next pool.

In a rams, however, the settlement is different. If the rams player wins all the tricks, she wins the whole pool plus five counters from every other player. If she loses a trick, the cards are at once thrown in; she must pay enough counters to double the pool and five counters to every player.

If everybody ahead of the player to the right of the dealer passes, this player must pay the dealer five counters if he wishes to drop. In this case, the pool remains undivided. If only one player other than the dealer decides to play, the dealer must play to defend the pool. In this case, he takes the trump card and discards another face down.

Sixty-Six

Players: 2.
Cards: 24 cards: Ace, King, Queen, Jack, 10 and 9 of each suit. (Discard all 2s to 8s.)

The Deal: Each player receives six cards, dealt three at a time. Place the rest of the pack face down in the middle of the table, to form the stock. Turn the top card of the stock face up and place it partly underneath the stock. This is the *trump card* and it decides the trump suit.
The Rank: The cards in each suit rank:

(Highest)  **(Lowest)**

Early Play: The non-dealer leads first. The cards are played out in tricks. A trick is won by the higher trump or by the higher card played of the suit led. The winner of a trick draws the top card of the stock, and the opponent draws the next card. In this way, each hand is restored to six cards after each trick.

During this early play, you do not have to follow suit to the lead. You may play any card. The early play ends when the stock is exhausted.

To Win the Game: You try to meld marriages (see below), win cards in tricks and win the last trick. The first player to reach a total of 66 or more points wins a game point. The first one to score seven *game points* wins an overall game.

Marriages: A marriage is meld of a King and Queen of the same suit. In the trump suit, a marriage counts 40. In any other suit, it counts 20. To score a marriage, you must show it after winning a trick, then lead one of the two cards.

If the non-dealer wants to lead a King or Queen from a marriage for an opening lead, she may show the marriage and then do so. But she may not score the marriage until after she has won a trick.

Trump Card: A player who has the 9 of trumps may exchange it for the trump card—to get a higher trump. He may make this exchange only after winning a trick, before making the next lead.

Closing: At any turn to lead, a player may turn the trump card face down. By doing that he closes—that is, stops—any further drawing from the stock. The hands are played out as in *Later Play* (see below), except that marriages may still be melded.

Later Play: After the stock is exhausted, you play out the six cards in each hand. In this part of the game, you must follow suit to the lead, if you can.

Counting Cards: Cards won in tricks are counted as follows:

Each Ace	**11**
Each 10	**10**
Each King	**4**
Each Queen	**3**
Each Jack	**2**
For winning the last trick	**10**

Scoring: Marriages are scored on paper whenever melded. Points taken in tricks are not entered on paper until a hand is finished, but it is important to keep mental track of these points and your opponent's points as they are won. In your turn to play, you may claim that you have reached 66. Then stop play at once and count. If you're right:

- **you score one *game point***
- **or two if your opponent has less than 33**
- **or three game points if he has not even won a trick.**

If you are wrong, and you don't have 66:

- **your opponent scores two game points.**

The reason it's so important to realize when you have won a game—and to claim it—is that you may lose by playing out the hand. If you and your opponent both get more than 66, or if you tie at 65, neither of you wins. But the winner of the next hand gets one additional game point.

Usually, at least one game point is won by somebody in each deal. As mentioned earlier, you win by scoring seven game points in an overall game.

Three-Hand Sixty-Six

Players: 3.
Cards: Same as in *Sixty-Six:* 24 cards,
Ace down to 9.

The Deal: The dealer gives six cards to the other two players, but deals none to himself.
The Play: The non-dealers play regular *Sixty-Six*.
Scoring: The dealer scores the same number of game

points as the winner of the deal. If both players get 66 or more—or tie at 65 (without a claim)—they score nothing and the dealer scores one. But a player is not allowed to win the overall game (seven points) when he is the dealer. If the usual scoring would put him up to seven points or over, his total becomes six, and he must win that last point as an active player.

Four-Hand Sixty-Six _____

Players: 4.
Cards: 32 cards from a regular pack. Ace, King, Queen, Jack, 10, 9, 8, and 7 of each suit. (Discard 2s through 6s.)

The Deal: Each player receives eight cards. The last card, turned face up for trump, is shown to each player, and then taken into the dealer's hand.
The Play: Players sitting opposite each other are partners. There is no melding. At all times you must follow suit to a lead, if possible, and also must, if possible, play higher than any card already played to the trick. When a plain suit is led and you have none, you must trump or overtrump if you can.
Scoring: Play out every hand. There is no advantage in claiming to have won. The winning side scores:

> **1 game point for having taken 66 to 99** or
> **2 game points for 100 to 129** or
> **3 game points for every trick (130).**

If the sides tie at 65, one extra game point goes to the side winning the next hand.

8.
The Whist Family

Back in the 1890's the games editor of an English magazine received a letter to this effect:

"My son, aged nine, has seen his elders playing *Whist* and now wishes to learn the game. Can you recommend to me some simple game I can teach him that will serve as an introduction to *Whist*?"

The editor replied, "Yes, I can recommend such a game. The game is *Whist*."

The fact is that the rules of *Whist* are simple and few. You can learn them in two minutes. *Whist* is just about the simplest of all card games to play *at*. What is not so easy is to play *Whist* well, for its extraordinary scope for skillful play lets the expert pull miles ahead of the beginner.

Whist

Players: 4, in partnerships.

Cards: Each receives 13 cards, dealt one at a time.

The Deal: The last card of the pack, belonging to the dealer, is exposed to all the players. This card decides the trump suit for that hand.

The Rank: In every suit the cards rank:

(**Highest**)   (**Lowest**)

The Play: The player to the left of the dealer makes the first lead. The hands are played out in tricks. You must *follow suit* to the lead if possible. Otherwise, you may play or lead as you please. However, if a player *revokes* by not following suit when he has in his hand an appropriate card to play, he and his partner have to pay a penalty. The penalty is decided upon before play begins, and may be as severe as two game points for the opponent. The partnership cannot win any trick in which it revokes.

A trick is won by the highest trump in it, or, if it contains no trump, by the highest card of the suit led. The winner of a trick makes the lead for the next trick.

One member of each partnership gathers together all the tricks won by his side. He doesn't throw them together in a single pile but overlaps them crosswise, so that each batch of four cards remains separate from the others.

To Win the Game: Win as many tricks as possible. Points for tricks and honors are accumulated, and the first side to reach a total of seven game points wins.

Scoring: The side that wins the majority of the tricks scores

1 game point for each trick over 6, and,

if agreed upon, 2 game points on the occasions when the opponents revoke.

In addition, points are scored for *honors*. The honors are the Ace, King, Queen and Jack of trumps.

If 2 honors were dealt to each side, there is no score.
If one side received 3 honors, it scores 2.
For all 4 honors, the score is 4.

Remember that honors are scored by the side to which they are *dealt*, not won in play. Both sides may score in the same deal, one side winning a majority of tricks and the other side holding a majority of honors.

Dummy Whist

Players: 3.
Cards: As in *Whist*.

The Deal: In this adaptation of *Whist* for three players, four hands are dealt, as usual, with the extra hand or "dummy" going opposite the dealer.

The Play: The same as in *Whist*, except that the dealer plays the dummy hand as well as his own against the two live opponents. Of course, the dealer must be careful to play each hand at its proper turn.

Scoring: The dealer has a great advantage over his opponents, since he gets to see all 26 cards on his side. The fairest scoring method is to play three, six or nine deals so that each player has the same number of turns to deal. Then the player with the highest score is declared the winner.

Bridge Whist

Players:	**4, in partnerships.**
Cards:	**Same as in _Whist_.**
Equipment:	**Score pad and pencil.**

This game is played in the same way as basic _Whist_, but it has a number of complications.

Trumps: No trump card is turned. The dealer may name trump, if he wishes, or he may pass. If he does pass, his partner must name the trump. Any of the four suits may be named trump, or the player may call "No trump," meaning that the hand will be played without a trump suit.

Doubles: After the trump—or no trump—is named, either one of the non-dealers may declare "I double." This multiplies the score of the winners by two.

After such a double, either member of the dealer's side may declare "I redouble" or "I double back." The teams may redouble alternately without limit, until one team quits. Then the cards are played.

The Play: After the opening lead by the player to the left of the dealer, the dealer's partner puts her cards face up on the table in vertical rows by suit. The dealer then plays the "dummy" as well as his own hand, just as in _Dummy Whist_.

Scoring: The score is kept on a score pad. The sheet is divided into two halves by a vertical line. All the scores for one team (WE) are entered in the left-hand column, and the scores of the other team (THEY) in the right. The sheet is also divided by a horizontal line, somewhat below the middle. Only odd trick scores are entered below the line, and they are accumulated to determine when a game has been won (total score of 30).

All other scores go above the line. When the play ends, each column is added up to determine the grand total won by each side, for odd tricks, honors, slams, rubbers. For instance, the score sheet may look like this:

	WE	THEY
Honors & → Bonuses	40 20 100	
Tricks → game 1 → game 2 → = A rubber	30 120	24

Scoring Tricks: The team winning at least six of the 13 tricks has a "book." It will score only tricks in excess of books of six. These score-able tricks are called *odd tricks*. Score them as follows:

If trumps were	♠	♣	♦	♥	No trump
Each odd trick would count	2	4	6	8	10

Each double that was made multiplies the score of the winners by two, each redouble by four.

Scoring Honors: Points are also scored for honors, which are written above the line on your score sheet. These are kept separate from points for tricks, which are written below the line.

The honor count is considerably more complicated than in *Whist*. When the game is played in a trump suit, the five top trumps—Ace, King, Queen, Jack and 10—become honors. You take the odd-trick value and multiply it by the number shown below to get the honor score, which gets written above the line.

> **Team with 3 honors or *chicane*** ×2
> (chicane is a hand without a trump)
> **4 honors divided between partners** ×4
> **4 honors in one hand** ×8
> **4 honors in one hand, 5th in partner's** ×9
> **5 honors in one hand** ×10

When you multiply this out, remember that the score you get is for honors only. It does not affect the scoring of the odd tricks, which you have already written below the line.

In a no-trump game, the honors are the four Aces. Score them as follows:

> **Team with 3 Aces** 30
> **4 Aces, divided** 40
> **4 Aces in one hand** 100

Scoring Bonuses: If one side wins all 13 tricks, it scores a bonus of 40 for *grand slam*. For winning 12 tricks, a *little slam*, there is a bonus of 20. These numbers get written above the line on your score pad.

To Win the Game: The first team to win 30 points in odd tricks wins a game. The team to win a *rubber*—two games—wins a bonus of 100 points, and *the* game.

Nullo Games

In order to win nullo games, you need to *avoid* winning tricks, or avoid taking certain cards in tricks. Most of the games are especially easy for children to learn because they have practically no other rules. Only in *Omnibus Hearts* do we find the added wrinkle that you *do* want to win some cards while you *don't* want to win others.

Four Jacks

Other Name: **Polignac**
Players: **4, 5 or 6.**
Cards: **With 4 players, 32 cards as follows: Ace, King, Queen, Jack, 10, 9, 8, 7—a full deck, but with all 2s to 6s discarded. All the 32 cards are dealt; each player receives 8 cards.**

   With 5 or 6 players, 30 cards—same as above but the two black 7s are also discarded. Each player receives 6 or 5 cards.
Equipment: **A handful of counters—poker chips, matchsticks, toothpicks, dried beans, etc. Distribute the same number to each player.**

The Play: The player to the left of the dealer leads first. The hands are played out in tricks. There is no trump suit. Each trick is won by the highest card played of the suit led.
To Win the Game: Avoid winning any Jacks. But before the opening lead, any player may announce that he will try to win all the tricks. This is called *capot.*
Scoring: Payments for holding Jacks and winning capot are made into a common pool, which is divided equally among all the players when the game ends. Whenever one

9.
The Hearts Family

This is the chief group of nullo games. In all of them, the way to win is to avoid winning Hearts.

If you are invited to play *Hearts* with a group that you have never played with before, it's a good idea to ask them to state the rules. Otherwise, you may find yourself playing one game while they play another.

The name of the basic game, *Hearts*, is used loosely for all its offspring, but there are many variations. *Black Maria* and *Black Lady* often denote games that are different from either the *Black Lady* or *Hearts* described here.

wins all the hearts. A good alternative is to deduct 13—(or 26, as agreed) from his score, preserving the principle that a player with a bad hand should have a chance to save himself (or gain) by taking *all* the Hearts.

Heartsette

This game adapts *Hearts* to an odd number of players.

Players: 3 or 5.
Cards: Place a *widow* (a group of cards) on the table—4 cards if 3 are playing, 2 cards if 5 are playing.

The Deal: Deal out the rest of the cards.
The Play: Play in the same way as *Hearts*, but the widow is turned face up after the first trick and goes to the winner of that trick. He must of course pay for any Hearts it contains.

Spot Hearts

This variation features a different scoring method that you can apply to any member of the *Hearts* family. The charges for ta. .ng Hearts go according to rank:

Ace counts	**14**
King counts	**13**
Queen counts	**12**
Jack counts	**11**
Others count	**face value**

Joker Hearts

This is *Hearts*, with a Joker added.

Players: **Same.**
Cards: **Add a Joker to the pack, discarding the 2 of Clubs to keep the deck at 52 cards.**

The Joker can be beaten only by the Ace, King, Queen or Jack of Hearts. Otherwise, it wins any trick to which it is played.

If you're playing *Heartsette*, deal an extra card to the widow.

The Joker counts as one Heart in payment or, in *Spot Hearts* scoring, 20.

Draw Hearts

This is *Hearts* for two players.

Players: **2.**
Cards: **13 to each player.**

The Deal: Place the rest of the deck face down in the middle of the table, forming the stock.
The Play: The cards are played in tricks. The winner of a trick draws the top card of the stock, and his opponent takes the next. After the stock is exhausted, the hands are played out without drawing.
To Win the Game: Take fewer Hearts.

Auction Hearts

The idea of this game is to let the players bid for the privilege of naming the suit to be avoided.

Each player in turn has one chance to bid, and the highest bidder names the "minus" suit.

Bids are made in numbers of counters that the player is willing to pay into the pool. Settlement is also made with counters, as in basic *Hearts*.

If the pool becomes a jackpot, there is no bidding in the next deal. The same player retains the right to name the minus suit, without further payment, until the jackpot is won. This player also makes the opening lead.

Domino Hearts

Players: **5 or 6.**
Cards: **Each receives 6 cards.**

The Deal: The rest of the pack is put face down in the middle of the table, forming the stock. All tricks must be composed of cards of the same suit—there is no discarding. When a player is unable to follow suit to the lead, he must draw from the stock until he gets a playable card. After the stock is exhausted, he must pass.

When a player's hand is exhausted, he drops out of the deal and the others play on. If he should win a trick with his last card, the player to his left leads for the next trick.

When all but one have dropped out, the last player must add his remaining cards to his own tricks.

Hearts taken are charged at one point each.

To Win the Game: Have the lowest total when another player reaches 31 points.

Black Lady

This is the best-known game of the *Hearts* family. It is what most people refer to when they speak of *Hearts*.

Players:	**3 to 7. It is best for 4, without partnerships.**
Cards:	**Deal out the whole pack, giving equal hands to all.**
	With 4 players it works out correctly.
	With 3 players, discard 1 deuce.
	With 5 players, discard 2 deuces.
	With 6 players, discard 4 deuces.
	With 7 players, discard 3 deuces.
Equipment:	**A handful of counters—poker chips, matchsticks, toothpicks, dried beans, etc.—the same amount to each player or: Pencil and paper for scoring.**

The Pass: After looking at his hand, each player passes any three cards he chooses to the player to his left. He must choose which cards he is going to pass and put them on the table before picking up the three cards passed to him by the player to his right.

The Play: The player to the left of the dealer makes the opening lead. The cards are played out in tricks. Aces rank highest. A trick is won by the highest card played of the suit led. The winner of a trick leads to the next trick.

To Win the Game: Avoid taking the Queen of Spades—called Black Lady, Black Maria, Calamity Jane, etc.—and avoid taking Hearts; or else take *all* the Hearts *and* the Queen of Spades, called "shooting the moon."

Scoring: If one player takes all 14 "minus" cards, he can subtract 26 points from his score. Some people play instead that 26 points are added to everyone else's score. Otherwise, one point is charged for each Heart won, and 13 points for the Queen of Spades. A running total score is kept for each player on paper. The first one to reach 100 or more loses the game, and the one with the lowest total at that time wins.

When playing with young children, you may want a shorter game. In this case, set the limit at 50.

An alternative method is to score with counters, settling after each hand. Payments are made into a pool, distributed equally to the players from time to time.

Strategy: See *Omnibus Hearts* (page 100–101).

Cancellation Hearts _____

This is a variation for 6 or more players.

Players: **6 or more.**
Cards: **2 packs shuffled together.**

The Deal: Deal the cards as far as they will go evenly. Put the extra cards face down on the table as a widow. This group of cards goes to the winner of the first trick.

The Play: You play the game exactly the same way as *Black Lady*, except:

1. When two identical cards, such as two Aces of Diamonds, are played in the same trick, they cancel each other out, ranking as zero. They cannot win the trick. As a result, if a deuce is led and all the higher cards of the suit played to a trick are paired and therefore cancelled, the deuce would win the trick!

2. When all cards of the suit led are cancelled, the cards stay on the table and go to the next winner of a trick. The same leader leads again.

Scoring: As in *Black Lady*. Counters make for easier scoring than paper and pencil.

Discard Hearts

This is *Black Lady*, except that the three cards are sometimes passed to the left and sometimes to the right. The best plan is to alternate. The pass often allows you to ruin your neighbor. Alternate passing gives her the chance to get back at you.

Omnibus Hearts

Many players regard this as the most interesting game of the Hearts family. It is the same as *Black Lady* with one addition. The Jack of Diamonds, or sometimes the 10, is a "plus" card, counting 10 *for* you if you win it.

As a result, in this game, each suit has its own character: Clubs are neutral, Diamonds contain the plus card, Spades contain the worst minus card, and all the Hearts are minus cards. A player who makes a "take-all" must win all 13 Hearts, the Queen of Spades and the Jack of Diamonds.

Strategy: The most dangerous cards to hold are high Spades—Ace, King, Queen—without enough lower cards to guard them. Pass such high Spades when you are dealt less than three lower Spades. Pass high Hearts if you can afford to, and if they look dangerous, but two *low* Hearts are usually enough to guard them. Any suit outside of Spades is dangerous if you have four or more without any card lower than, say, a six. Even a single very low card—a two or a three—may not be a sufficient guard. Pass one to three cards from the top or middle of such a suit, if you do not have more pressing troubles.

If you do not have any high Spades after the pass, lead Spades at every opportunity. You can never gather Black Maria by a lower Spade lead! You want to try to force her out by Spade leads so that you can save yourself from winning her by discard. If you have her yourself, it is usually best to lead your shortest side suit so as to get rid of it and get the chance to discard Black Maria.

If you are dealt the Jack of Diamonds, pass it if you can afford to. The Jack is much easier to *catch* than to *save*. It is not often caught by higher Diamonds—and when it is, it is mostly by accident. It usually falls to the winner of the last trick. The hand with which you may hope to catch it has some Aces and Kings, adequately guarded by lower cards, in two or more suits. Of course, if you hope to catch the Jack, don't pass any higher Diamonds, and don't ever lead Diamonds if you can avoid it. But put a *high* Diamond on any Diamond lead that might be won by the Jack if you were to play low.

Don't attempt a take-all without a very powerful hand. Certain holdings are fatal no matter how strong you are in other suits—low Hearts, for example (not at the end of a long solid suit), and the Jack of Diamonds (without enough diamond length and strength to save the Jack even if you do not go for take-all). However, if you've got one or two middling-high Hearts, it is not fatal. You may be able to win the tricks simply by leading these Hearts. The players holding higher Hearts may shrink from taking the tricks.

When your chief ambition is to avoid taking minus cards, which is most of the time, get rid of your high cards early rather than late. Thus, if you have:

put the Ace on the *first* Club lead and the Jack on the *second*, saving your 2 to escape having to win the more dangerous third lead. The more often a suit is led, the more likely it becomes that Black Maria or Hearts will be discarded on it.

10.
Solitaire (Patience) Games

Solitaire games help pass the time pleasantly when you want to relax or when you have to stay in bed. Children enjoy them as much as adults, and they can provide hours of entertainment.

Accordion

Cards: 1 pack.

The Play: Deal the cards one at a time face up in a row from left to right. Go slowly so that you can continually compare the last card dealt with its neighbors. Whenever this card matches its neighbor immediately to the left, or the card third to its left, you may move the new card onto the card it matches.

The matching may be in suit or in rank.

Suppose the first four cards you turn up are:

The 6 of Diamonds matches the 6 of Clubs and also the Jack of Diamonds. You may move it over upon either card. Here, it is just a guess which play will turn out better. You may often find that one play is better because it opens up additional plays.

Keep watching for new plays that become possible when you consolidate the piles. For example, suppose that you deal:

You can move the 2 of Clubs onto the 2 of Hearts. Then, because the two Clubs are next to each other, you can move the 5 of Clubs onto the 2.

Move the piles of cards as a whole, not just the top card. When a gap is left in the row because you have moved a pile away, shove all the piles to the left to close up the gap.

To Win the Game: Get the whole pack into one pile. You will not succeed very often. You can really consider it a "win" if you end up with no more than five piles.

Hit or Miss

Cards: 1 pack.

The Play: Deal the cards one at a time face up into a single wastepile. As you deal, count "Ace, two, three..." and so on up to the King. Whenever the card you deal is the same as the rank you call, that is a *hit*. Throw all the hit cards out of the deck. After you count "King," start over again with "Ace, two..." and so on. When you have dealt the entire deck, pick up the wastepile, turn it face down, and continue dealing. Also continue counting from where you left off.

To Win the Game: Hit every card in the deck. But you lose the game if you go through the deck twice in succession without a single hit.

Even Up

Cards: 1 pack.
Preparation: **Discard all picture cards—Kings, Queens and Jacks.**

The Play: Shuffle the 40 cards that are left; then deal them one at a time face up in a row from left to right. Keep watching the pairs of adjacent cards. Whenever the members of a pair are both odd (such as two 7s) or both even (such as two 8s), throw them out.

To Win the Game: Throw out all 40 cards in pairs.

Knockout

Other Name: Hope Deferred
Cards: 1 pack.
Preparation: Discard all 2s to 6s, leaving a pack of 32 cards.

The Deal: Shuffle the 32-card pack well, and then deal three cards face up in a column at your left. If any is a Club, throw it out to start a wastepile and deal a new card to take its place. If the new card is a Club, throw it out and deal another—and so on—until you have three non-Clubs in the column.

The Play: Deal four more columns next to the first, from left to right, each containing three cards.

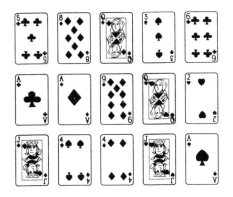

From this array of 15 cards, throw all Clubs into the wastepile. But do not fill the spaces you made in the four columns to the right of the first.

Gather the remaining cards of the array and shuffle them together with the cards left in the stock. In other words, shuffle all of the 32 cards except the discarded Clubs.

Deal a second time in the same way as the first, and again throw out all Clubs.

Gather the remainder, shuffle, and deal a third time.

To Win the Game: You must discard all eight Clubs in the three deals.

The Wish

I am reliably informed that if you win this game the first time you try it, you will get your wish. I cannot vouch for this, but that is what they say.

Cards: **1 pack.**
Preparation: **Discard all 2s to 6s, leaving a pack of 32 cards.**

The Play: Shuffle the 32-card pack well and count off four cards *face down*. Then turn them face up. Be careful to keep the pile squared up so that you cannot see the faces of any cards below the top.

    Deal the whole deck into piles of four cards in this way.

Then lift off the top cards in pairs of the same kind—two 7s, two Queens, and so on. Keep going as long as you see any pairs.

To Win the Game: You must clear away all the piles in pairs.

The Clock

Cards: **1 pack.**

The Deal: Shuffle the deck and then deal it into 13 piles of four cards each. Arrange 12 of the piles in a circle, to represent the numbers on a clock dial. Put the 13th pile in the middle of the circle.

The Play: Pick up the top card of the 13-pile. Suppose it is a 5. Shove it face up under the 5-pile and pick up the top card of that pile. Suppose it is a Jack. Put it under the 11-pile. Pick up the top of that pile—and so on.

Jacks represent 11, Queens 12, and Kings 13; other cards their face value.

To Win the Game: You must get all the cards face up. The game is lost if you come to the fourth King before all the other cards have been moved face up to their proper "hour" piles.

Klondike

Other Name: **Patience**
Cards: **1 pack.**

The Deal: Deal a row of seven cards, the first (at the left) face up and the others face down.

Next, deal a card face up on the second pile and one face down on each of the piles to the right.

Continue with a card face up on the third pile and cards face down on every pile to the right.

And keep on dealing in the same way until you end up with one card face up on the last pile to the right. Thus, each pile has one additional card in it, the top card of each pile is face up, and all the others are face down. The rest of the cards are left on the side, face down, as the stock.

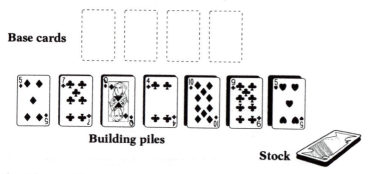

Base cards

Building piles

Stock

The Play: You may move the face-up cards to build them on each other. In building, you need to alternate colors—red on black or black on red—and go down in rank. That means the 4 of Clubs may be moved onto the 5 of Hearts or onto the 5 of Diamonds. Kings are highest and may be moved only into spaces created by removing entire piles.

In building, keep the cards spread downwards as in the illustration, so that you can read them all. When two or more cards are built on each other, move all of them as a unit. For example, if you have a black 10 on a red Jack, you may move the two cards together onto a black Queen. Whenever you move a face-up card off a pile, turn up the top face-down card.

Aces are *base* cards. Whenever you have an Ace on a pile, or turn an Ace up from stock, put it in a *base* row above the piles. Build up on the Aces in suit and sequence from Ace to King.

To Win the Games: You must get all four suits built up on the Aces.

After you have done all the building you can on the piles and on the Aces, if any, turn over the top card of the *stock* (the undealt remainder of the deck). Play this card onto a pile or a base if you can. If you can't, set it aside face up to start your wastepile.

Continue turning up cards from the stock one by one, playing them when you can and putting them on the wastepile when you can't. You may play off the top of the wastepile, if such a play becomes possible.

Go through the stock only once.

Strategy: You must put Aces in the base row whenever they turn up, but you don't have to build on them every time you get the chance. It sometimes pays to keep cards on the piles instead of moving them to bases, in order to help in building.

The important thing is to uncover all the face-down cards as quickly as possible. When, for instance, you have a choice of which play to make (say you have black 9s on two piles and a red 10 opens up), it's usually a good idea to select the 9 from the pile that has the most face-down cards.

You may prefer, however, to reach a single face-down card, since you will open up a space if you can get it out of the way. It is helpful to get spaces when you can, because that's the only way you can move a King. If you don't open up spaces, the Kings that you have will stay where they are and prevent you from reaching the face-down cards underneath them.

Variation

Instead of turning over one card at a time from stock you may turn over the cards in packs of three. You then have the right to go through the stockpile as many times as you want.

Canfield

Cards: 1 pack.

The Deal: Count off 13 cards face down and put them on the table at your left, face up. Keep the pile squared up so that you can only read the top card.

Deal one card face up on the table, above and to the right of the 13-pile. This card is your first *base*, and all other cards of the same rank will also be bases. Whenever you uncover any base card, you will move it up into a row beside the first.

Deal four cards in a row face up to the right of the 13-pile. These cards start your building piles.

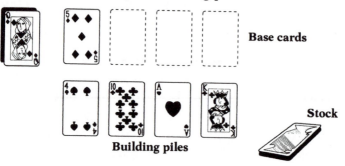

Base cards

Building piles

Stock

The Play: Build as in Klondike, down in rank and alternating in color. But your base cards are not necessarily Aces, as in *Klondike*. The rank of cards goes "around the corner"—

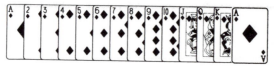

starting from the base card. Suppose this is a 5. Then 4s cannot be moved off the piles except to be built on the bases. Kings are no problem, however. They may be built upon Aces.

To Win the Game: You must get the whole pack built up on the four base cards.

Whenever you open up a space by clearing away one of the building piles, fill the space with the top card of the 13-pile. It is vital to dig into the 13-pile as quickly as possible. Build up in suit and sequence on your base cards, as in *Klondike*, remembering to "go around the corner" when the bases are not Aces.

The undealt remainder of the deck is the stock. Turn up cards from the stock in batches of three, being careful not to mix their order. Lay each batch of three on a single waste-pile. The top card of each batch may be played upon the piles or bases, and lower cards in the wastepile may be played off as soon as they are uncovered. Go through the whole stockpile by threes, playing what you can. Then turn the wastepile face down to form a new stockpile, and go through it by threes again. This way, you may run through the stock without limit—until you win the game or come to a standstill.

After your 13-pile is exhausted (all the cards having been played into spaces, put on the building piles, or put on the bases), you may fill a space in the building piles with any available card you please. Don't be too hasty about filling those precious spaces. You may need them to uncover key cards in your stock. It is a good idea to fill a late space only when you think that you will be able to get the space back again before the game is blocked.

Pounce _____

Other Name: **Racing Demon**
Players: **2 to 8. The only limit is the number that can sit around the table and find playing space and elbow room.**

Cards:	As many packs as there are players. All the packs must have different backs so that the cards can be sorted out later.

This is a way of playing *Klondike* or *Canfield* as a round game.

The Deal: Each player has his or her own deck. Each player lays out the cards for *Klondike* or *Canfield*—whatever game is chosen. Everybody must be given time to complete the layout. Then, at a signal, all begin to play.

To Win the Game: The first player to get rid of all his cards onto the bases wins the game.

The Play: Each plays the game in the usual way, building on his own piles, but all the base cards must be put in the middle of the table and they become everybody's property. A player may build on anybody's base cards.

If the play comes to a standstill before any of the players have gotten rid of all their cards, the base piles are sorted out and the cards are returned to their owners. The one who got the most cards onto the bases wins the game.

The game is very exciting, and the few rules need to be enforced strictly to keep it from getting rough. A player may put cards on the bases with one hand only—the right hand, if the person is right-handed. If several players try to put the same card on the same pile simultaneously, the one whose card is lowest wins the race and all the others must be taken back.

A Shorter Game

When the game is *Canfield*, you can play a shorter game in which the winner is the first one to get rid of the 13-card pile. It doesn't matter where the cards go—onto the bases or onto the building piles, so long as they are moved *somewhere*.

Beehive

This is essentially *Canfield* with simplified building.

Cards: 1 pack.

The Deal: Count off 10 cards face down; then place them face up on the table at your left. This is the *beehive*. To the right of the hive, deal six cards face up, in any convenient arrangement, such as two rows of three. These cards are the *garden*.

Beehive

Garden

The Play: The building is by rank; that is, a 9 goes on a 9, a Queen on a Queen, and so on. Build only on the garden, never on the hive. But remove the top card of the hive whenever you can, to put it on the garden. Garden cards or piles may be built together when they are of the same rank.

Whenever you make a space in the six places reserved for the garden, move the top card of the hive into the space, thus releasing the next card of the hive.

The undealt remainder of the deck is the stock. As in *Canfield*, go through the stock in batches of three cards at a time, being careful not to disturb the order of the cards. Put each batch face up on a single wastepile. You may play off the wastepile onto the garden.

After exhausting the stock, pick up your wastepile without shuffling it, turn it over to form a new stock, and go through it again. You may continue going through the stock-wastepile without limit, until you win the game or are blocked.

Whenever you get all four cards of a rank together in the garden, throw out this pile, creating a space. After the beehive is exhausted, you may fill spaces from the wastepile.

To Win the Game: Throw out the whole pack in fours of the same rank.

Gaps

Cards: 1 pack.

The Deal: Deal out the whole pack face up, in four rows of 13 cards each.

To Win the Game: You need to get all four suits in order, one to each row, from 2 to King, going from left to right.

The Play: Pick out the four Aces and discard them, leaving *gaps* in the rows. Examine the card to the left of each gap. You may move the next-higher card of the same suit into the gap.

For example, if the 8 of Diamonds is to the left of a gap, you may move in the 9 of Diamonds. Moving in the 9 of Diamonds will leave a gap that you may then fill in the same way with the card that is next higher in rank than the card to the left of the gap.

Whenever a gap is created at the left end of a row, fill it with any deuce you please.

When a King lies to the left of a gap, that gap is dead; you cannot fill it. When all four gaps go dead, gather up all the cards—except for the Aces, which have already been discarded—and the cards that are in proper sequence with a 2 at the left end of a row. Shuffle the cards well and deal them again, so as to re-make the four rows of 13, but leave a gap in each row just to the right of the cards that were not gathered up. That allows you to bring one additional card into its proper place in each row, to start you on a new series of plays.

When play again becomes blocked, gather up the cards again and redeal in the same way. You are allowed three deals in all.

Strategy: Make the most of the choice you have in play. Choice often arises in the *order* of moving cards, and in the selection of a 2 to fill a left-end gap. It is surprising how often a good choice will open up many more plays than a poor one.

Pirate Gold

Cards: 1 pack.

The Deal: Deal 10 cards face up on the table. You may place them in any convenient array, such as two rows of five cards each.

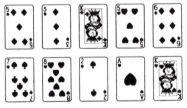

The Play: If any two of these cards are a pair (two Kings, two 5's, etc.), cover each one with another face-up card from the deck. Continue in the same way, dealing cards so as to cover all the pairs you see.

To Win the Game: You must succeed in dealing out the whole deck.

The game comes out most of the time, but once in a while you will find yourself blocked with all ten cards in sight of different ranks. In fact, when *I* played the game as a boy, I turned it around: I considered that I won *only* if a block arose, so I did not *have* to deal out the whole deck to cover all the pairs.

Pyramid

Cards: 1 pack.

The Deal: Deal 28 cards face up in the form of a pyramid. Start with one card at the top, then a row of two below it with these cards overlapping the lower corners of the first. Continue with a row of three overlapping the row of two, and so on, ending with a row of seven at the bottom. Thus, each card in the upper rows is overlapped by two cards in the row just below it.

The Play: At the beginning, only the seven car[ds in the]
bottom row are free to be moved away. As thes[e are]
moved, cards in the next row up become free.

Whenever you see two free cards in the pyram[id that]
total 13, you may remove them to a discard pile. Jack [(count-]
ing 11) makes 13 with a 2, and Queen (counting 12) go[es with]
an Ace (1). Kings count 13 and so may be removed [at will.]
Begin the play by removing what cards you can fro[m the]
pyramid.

The undealt remainder of the pack is the stock. [Put it]
face down at your left, with the discard pile at your r[ight.]
Turn up cards from the top of the stock one at a time. W[hen]
you cannot use a turned card immediately, put it face u[p in]
a wastepile between the stock and discard pile. You m[ay]
play off the top of the wastepile, just as you can play fr[om]
the pyramid.

If a card turned from the stock makes 13 with a fre[e]
card of the pyramid, or with the top card of the wastepile[,]
you may remove such cards to the discard pile.

To Win the Game: Get the whole deck into the discard
pile—that is, match all the cards into 13s.

It is perfectly all right to keep the wastepile spread so
that you can see all the cards in it. When you have the choice
of removing a card from the wastepile or the pyramid, try to
calculate whether one play or the other will cause a block.

For example, suppose that three 7s are gone, two into
the discard and one into the wastepile. You turn up the
fourth 7, and there happen to be free 6s on the wastepile and
on the pyramid. If you take the 6 from the pyramid, you will
be blocked, for the 7 needed to remove the 6 from the
wastepile is buried below it. Therefore you must use the
fourth 7 to play from the wastepile, hoping to be able to
uncover the buried 7 to match with the 6 on the pyramid.

imple Addition

nless you are much luckier than I am, you will not win
yramid often. When you find yourself blocked for the ump-
eenth time, give it up and try *Simple Addition*. The princi-
le is the same but you don't have to contend with all those
uried cards!

Cards: 1 pack.

The Deal: Deal 10 cards face up, in two rows of five.

The Play: Remove two cards at a time that total 13—
Queen with Ace, Jack with 2, 10 with 3, and so on. Remove
Kings alone. Fill the spaces by dealing additional cards
from the deck.

To Win the Game: Throw out the whole deck in 13s. You
are bound to win if you succeed in dealing out the entire
deck.

Lazy Boy

Cards: 1 pack.

The Deal: Shuffle the deck well. Turn it face down and

take off three cards from the top, without disturbing their order. Put this batch of three face up on the table to start your wastepile. If the top card is an Ace or King, remove it to a row above the wastepile. Eventually you must get all the Aces and Kings into two rows above the wastepile, forming the bases.

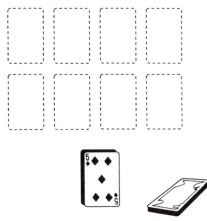

The Play: On the Aces, build cards of the same suit upwards in sequence from Ace to 7. On the Kings, build downwards in the same suit from King to 8.

Go through the entire deck, turning over batches of three cards at a time and putting the batches on the wastepile. Play off the top card of this pile when you can, either to put a base card (Ace or King) in place or to play on a base pile. The lower cards in the wastepile become available for play when they become uncovered.

Once you have exhausted the stock, pick up the wastepile, turn it over, and continue as before. Be careful not to shuffle or disturb the order of the cards in the wastepile. You may run through the stock as many times as you please, until you have won the game or it has become blocked.

To Win the Game: Build the whole deck onto the base cards.

Four-Leaf Clover

It is said that you will have good luck all day if you win this game.

Cards: 1 pack.

The Deal: Discard all four 10s from the deck—they are not used in the game. Shuffle the remaining 48 cards well. Then deal 16 cards face up on the table in four rows of four each.

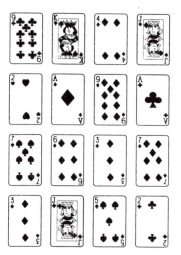

The Play: Whenever you can, throw out from this layout any two or more cards *of the same suit,* as follows:

   1. Two or more cards that total 15, such as 9 and 6 or 8-4-2-Ace (Ace counts as one).

   2. Three cards: the King, Queen or Jack.

After you throw out a batch of cards, deal from the deck to fill the spaces left in the 16-card layout.

To Win the Game: Throw out all 48 cards. Another way of saying it is that you must succeed in dealing out the entire deck, for if you do, the final 16 cards are bound to match up properly.

Strategy: In making 15s, try to remove as many cards as possible, so as to bring in all the new cards you can.

Perpetual Motion

Cards: 1 pack.

The Deal: Deal four cards face up in a row from left to right. If any are of the same rank (such as 6s, Aces, Jacks, etc.) move the others upon the one farthest left. Then deal four more cards from left to right on the four piles (counting a space as a pile if you have moved any of the first four cards). Play in the same way if you can, moving any two or more cards of the same rank upon the leftmost such card. All these moves must be one card (the top card) at a time; do not move a whole pile at once.

Continue dealing the deck four cards at a time on the previous piles, making what moves you can each time.

Once you have exhausted the deck, pick up the pile from right to left. That is, put Pile Four (at the right), still face up, on Pile Three (at its left); put these two together on Pile Two, and then all of it on Pile One. Be careful not to disturb the order of the cards. Then turn the whole pile face down, forming a new stockpile. Go through it again. You may deal out the stock as many times as you please, until you finally win the game or are blocked.

Whenever the four cards you deal at one time are of the same rank, throw them out, reducing the size of the stock.
To Win the Game: Throw out the entire deck in batches of four of a rank.

You will see why the game is called *Perpetual Motion* the first time you play it. It really should be classed as an athletic game!

Russian Bank

Players: 2.
Cards: Each player has a regular pack of 52 cards. The two decks must have different backs.

The Deal: Each player deals from her own deck a pile of 12 cards face down. She puts it to her right.

Above the 12-card pile, she deals a line of four cards, face up, extending towards her opponent. These eight cards (four from each player) start the building piles and they are common property.

She then puts the undealt remainder of the deck face down to her left—that is her stock.

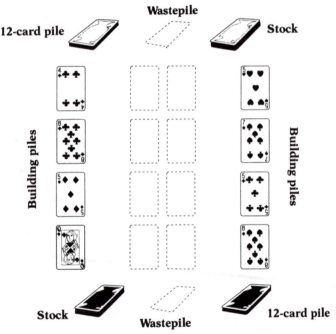

Bases: All Aces are base cards. When Aces become available, they must be moved into the middle of the table and set up in two columns, parallel to the building piles.

The players may build cards on the Aces—cards in the same suit and in upward sequence—from 2 to King.

Building Piles: Players may also build on these piles—downwards and in alternating colors, as in *Klondike* and *Canfield*. For instance, the 4 of Clubs may be moved onto the 5 of Hearts or the 5 of Diamonds. The Jack of Hearts could be moved onto any black Queen, and so on. A King cannot be built on another card in the building piles, but it may, of course, go on a Queen of the same suit on one of the base piles.

Only one card at a time may be moved to and from the building piles. (This is different from *Klondike* and *Canfield*, where the whole pile is moved as a unit.)

The Play: Players take turns; you do not play simultaneously, as in *Pounce*.

At the very first turn of the play, the player must move any Aces from the building piles into the base positions, and also any other cards—2s or 3s, for example—that may be built on them. Only after that may she turn the top card of her 12-card pile face up. With the exception of this very first turn, a player begins her turn with at least one card face up on her 12-card pile.

It is very important to observe the following rules in the *order* of play; otherwise, you can lose your turn.

Rules of Order: An *available* card is one that is free to be moved. The word "available" covers:

- **the top card of each building pile**
- **the top card of the player's 12-card pile**
- **a card turned up from the player's stock but not yet put on her wastepile.**

The cards in the wastepile are *never* available. Nor is any card that is covered by another in a building pile, though it may *become* available should the covering card be moved. You cannot be charged with an error because you could have made a lower card available but did not.

1. Whenever you can move an available card to the bases, you must make this move before any other.

2. If a card from the 12-card pile can be played to the bases, this play must be made ahead of a move from a building pile to the bases.

3. On clearing face-up cards off the 12-card pile, you must turn up the top face-down card *before making any other move.*

4. You may move available cards from the building piles to the bases in any order.

5. Once you have made all possible moves to the bases, you are free to manipulate the building piles as you please to make additional cards available, create spaces, and so on.

A space is created whenever all the cards in one building pile are removed. As spaces open up, you are allowed to move any available card into them from a building pile.

For example, let's say that one pile is made up of a 9 of Clubs and an 8 of Diamonds. There is a 10 of Hearts on another pile, and there is a space. Were you to move the 8 of Diamonds into the space, you could uncover the 9 of Clubs and move it onto the 10 of Hearts. Then, when you put the 8 of Diamonds back on the 9 of Clubs, you have *two* spaces instead of one. Look for such opportunities to create spaces, because they help you get rid of your own cards.

6. You must move the top card of your 12-card pile—as long as it lasts—into a space before you may play from your stock into spaces.

7. You must fill all spaces in the building piles before turning up a card from your stock.

Having fulfilled all the *Rules of Order*, a player may then turn up the top card of her stock. She must play it to the bases if possible. If not, she may put it on a building pile. (See also *Loading*.) If she can't find a space for it anywhere, she must put it face up on her wastepile, and this act ends her turn. Her turn continues as long as she can find a place for the cards she turns up from her stock. Whenever a player places a card on her wastepile, her turn ends, even if there was actually a place where she could have played it.

Loading: You may build available cards not only on the base cards and the building piles, but also upon your opponent's 12-card pile and his wastepile. This is called *loading* him. On his cards, you must build in suit and sequence, but the sequence may go up or down or both ways, as you please.

For example, if his 12-card pile shows a Jack of Diamonds, you may move an available 10 onto it. Should you then turn up a Jack of Diamonds from your own stock, you can put it on the 10 of Diamonds.

There is no advantage in loading your opponent from the building piles alone, because he can build the cards right back when his turn comes. But if you can cover such cards with one from your stock or your 12-card pile, that's splendid—for you! You have gotten rid of some cards and have loaded him with some more to get rid of.

Stopping: If a player violates any of the *Rules of Order*, her opponent may call "Stop!" If he can prove she made an error, her turn ends.

In a very strict game, you can be stopped if you so much as touch a card when you should move another one first. A fairer rule is that a Stop may not be called until a player has actually picked up a wrong card.

When a player's stock is exhausted, she must immediately turn over her wastepile to form a new stock. When her 12-card pile is exhausted, she continues without it, playing from her stock.

To Win the Game: The first player to get rid of her entire 12-card pile and stock wins the game. She scores 30 points for winning, plus two points for each card left in her opponent's 12-card pile and one point for each card in his stock and wastepile.

What the Terms Mean

Around the corner: Refers to the ranking of the cards. Ace can be high and low.

Ante up: To put counters into the pool, so that they may be won during the game.

Base cards: In solitaire, refers to scoring cards, usually but not always Aces, which are built up to complete a set, usually a full 13-card suit.

Bidding: Stating what you are willing to pay or predicting the number of tricks you hope to win.

Book: The basic number of tricks bid. In *Whist*, the first six tricks won. In *Authors*, four cards of the same rank.

Capot: Trying to win all the tricks.

Chicane: A hand without a trump card in it.

Deuce: A 2 of any suit.

Follow suit: Put down a card that matches the suit of the lead.

Gin: To lay down your whole melded hand, face up, ending the play.

Honor card: Ace, King, Queen, Jack of trumps, and sometimes the 10.

Knock: To lay down all melds and declare the face value of unmelded cards.

Lead: The first play that establishes the suit to follow.

Marriage: A meld of King and Queen in the same suit.

Meld: To match up three or four cards of a kind or in sequence. Can be held in hand or put down on the table. A matched set.

Nullo games: Games in which you must avoid taking certain cards.

Picture card: Jack, Queen or King.

Revoke: Not following suit when you could have and were supposed to.

Spot cards: Any card from 2 to 10.

Suits: There are four: Hearts, Diamonds, Clubs and Spades.

Sweep: In Casino, capturing all the cards on the table in one play.

Trick: A sequence of cards in which each person plays a card according to certain rules.

Trump suit: A named suit that can overtake others, chosen in a specific way for each game.

Upcard: The top card of the stock, turned over beside the stockpile, which starts the discard pile.

Widow: An extra hand or number of cards that may be substituted for a player's own hand or held until a certain point in the game. Also, extra cards taken with the first tricks in Hearts.

Wild cards: Cards that prior to the game may be given any value you choose.

Index